A MEDDLING PRIEST

John Joseph Therry

By

John McSweeney PE

ST PAULS

First published in Australia in July 2000 by

ST PAULS PUBLICATIONS
60–70 Broughton Road — PO Box 230
Strathfield NSW 2135
http://www.stpauls.com.au

National Library of Australia
Cataloguing-in-publication data:

McSweeney, John
A Meddling Priest — John Joseph Therry

ISBN 1 876295 32 5

1. Therry, John Joseph, 1790–1864. 2. Catholic Church —
Australia — Clergy — Biography. 3. Priests — Australia —
Biography. I. Title. II. Title: John Joseph Therry.

282.092

Cover and colour sections designed by Graphic by Design,
    Erina NSW 2250
Printed by Ligare Pty Ltd, Riverwood NSW 2210
Typeset by Turn-Key Systems Pty Ltd, St Leonards NSW 2065

ST PAULS PUBLICATIONS is an activity of the priests and
brothers of the Society of St Paul who place at the centre of
their lives the mission of evangelisation through the modern
means of social communications.

CONTENTS

ACKNOWLEDGMENTS

I am indebted to the many people whose support and encouragement made this work possible. Ted Kennedy has generously shared with me the fruit of his own considerable research and has been an enthusiastic promoter of the project. Shirely Spinks has patiently and lovingly typed and re-typed the numerous drafts. Peter Finneran (formerly director OMP productions) has donated his considerable expertise and made the necessary connections to get the printing and designing done on time. My Parish Priest (Terry Brady) and staff have been constantly generous and reassuring. Professor Finbarr Donovan (Dublin University) has researched Therry's Cork ministry and Kevin O'Neill (Rector, Carlow College) has unearthed some helpful material from the College archives. Ed Campion (Chair, Literary Council of Australia), Martin Coleman (Irish Communications Council), MMK O'Sullivan (author) and Michael O'Sullivan (Chaplain, Irish National Association) have taken the time to read the draft, and as well as being very encouraging, have made good use of the editorial red pen. Terry Southerwood has gone over the Tasmanian chapters and made some helpful corrections and suggestions. Michael Goonan (St Paul's) has done some very useful editing. Mario Villareal, Matthew Botaro and Robert Spinks have generously donated their computer skills. I'm also indebted to the Veech Library, Cooma Cottage Yass, Fathers Fennell and Crahan and others who lent me books, some of which are now out of print.

The original inspiration for this project came from Joe Walsh PE (Castle Hill), Bishop David Cremin, Dean Tony Doherty (St Mary's Cathedral), an tAthair Micheál Ó Suilleabháin and the All Hallows On-going Committee.

Gradually and painfully taking shape at the same time as the new spires on St Mary's Cathedral, I pray this modest work will, like the spires, bring the Therry inspiration *urbi et orbi* (to the city and to the world).

John McSweeney
June, 2000

PROLOGUE

On arrival in Sydney from Ireland towards the end of World War II, I was delighted to hear that a fellow Corkman, Fr John Joseph Therry, who had preceded me by 125 years, was held in such high esteem. Revered by clergy and laity alike, he was pointed out to young curates as a model we could well emulate in our pastoral ministry. To the teachers and children in parish schools, he held the status of folk hero. I even saw his rather stern picture, with strong square chin prominent, decorating the occasional sitting or dining room in people's homes. It wasn't unusual to find him referred to in sermons and occasional talks, and snippets about him would grace Catholic magazines, even the *Catholic Weekly*, from time to time.

People were quite proud of their pioneer priest. I think they felt he encapsulated many of the qualities that were highly regarded in Australia. For example, he could live, as they say, on the smell of an oil rag and give his last penny to the poor. He stood up to the highest in the land on behalf of the powerless and voiceless. He was the friend of the convict and the Aborigine, and was often their only friend. Even though he fought with Bishops and other priests, he was a practical ecumenist before ecumenism was mainstream. He was deep in debt most of his life, while at the same time building more churches than anyone who came after him. He was said to suffer from a "lack of management in temporal affairs", and yet he acquired more land and showed more entrepreneurial skill than any of his successors.

Therry had all the qualities of which heroes and saints are made. His life story has the ingredients of a great mini-series: drama, heroism, conflicts, misunderstandings ... On his own and unaided, he is credited with having laid the foundations of the Catholic Church in Australia. And yet, as we begin the 21st century, his name has fallen out of circulation. His key place in the Australian Church is mostly ignored. Our children know the names of the great explorers, the Governors, and other leading figures of early Australiana, but the name John Joseph Therry scarcely strikes a chord with them.

Everyone knows that St Mary's Cathedral, Sydney, is Australia's first Catholic church — but the fact that Therry was the one who procured the site and built the first St Mary's is a best-kept secret.

The response and affirmation of ordinary Australians on the occasion of the 1995 beatification of Mother Mary McKillop had the surprising effect of drawing closer together people of different persuasions or of none. I believe the exhuming of John Joseph Therry from the Limbo to which he has been consigned would have a similar effect.

St Mary's Cathedral is now completed, with new twin spires. Were John Joseph Therry to join Mary McKillop, the spires could be symbols of these twin heroes of the Australian Church, lifting the hopes and dreams of all Australians at the dawn of a new millennium, a very special time, indeed.

In 1922, Dr (later Archbishop) Eris O'Brien put together a fine biography of Therry. Well researched and written with sincerity and clarity, it is, as far as I know, the only biography of Therry. Inevitably somewhat dated in style and in physical bulk, it has been out of print for years. Moreover, at the time it was written, some of the relevant data now at hand was unavailable to the author.

Recently, historians, Catholic and non-Catholic, professional and otherwise, have studied Therry's life and times in some detail, as part of general Australian Catholic history. They are deserving of all sorts of medals for the time and effort they have expended researching the voluminous Therry papers, not to mention all the other documents that refer to Therry.

In this scenario where just about every word of this prolific writer of letters, articles, memos, diaries etc, has been preserved and where everything written or said about him, no matter what the circumstances, has likewise been preserved, biographers have to be rather circumspect.

Therry was a very high-profile, rather flamboyant public figure in the New Holland (Australia) and Van Diemen's Land (Tasmania) of his time. He was, perhaps, the original Aussie Battler; so much so that in today's parlance, we would suspect he had a battling gene! Naturally, he ruffled many feathers. In his own time he was hated and he was loved; he was held up as a super folk-hero, and, maybe more than anyone else in his time, he was reviled, abused and denigrated. Extrapolating the latter view from the Therry papers and exposing it to public scrutiny without full contextual explanation, is dangerous.

An author (including this author) has his or her own, perhaps undisclosed, agendas, personal prejudices, and unique way of interpreting the written or reported word. Authors can make or break their subjects. Certainly some, maybe unwittingly, have badly damaged Therry among contemporary people.

Some authors present the pioneer priest in a very favourable light, more or less along the same lines as Eris O'Brien; some are much more critical. Although they take great care to set him on a fairly high pedestal, they quickly proceed to shoot him down, if not in flames, at least somewhat badly singed. One author, James Waldersee, who was rather critical of those he felt were too soft on Therry, set out to demonstrate that all his problems were of his own making and that people he had problems with were victims of the rebel priest's lack of caution and his truculence! This author allows Therry's most strident opponents to do their damnedest to bring "the disgraced Therry" to heel.

High profilers, or "tall poppies" being, like the rest of us, a complex mixture of light and darkness and various shades in between, are attractive targets for writers and researchers — especially those who have a gift and a yen for "cutting down to size". It would be rather tragic however, to let the darkness, the negative, prevail if we're convinced, as in the case of Therry, that the light, the positive, played the dominant role in his life. Even fellow priest and competent historian Terry Southerwood sailed a bit close to the wind when he published some scathing remarks about Therry, reportedly made at what seems to me to have been a private clerical conversation in the Hobart Bishop's residence.

In such situations clerics, like other people, tend to talk off the cuff and, in hurt or in frustration or even in humour, say things bluntly or without the usual nuances, things not intended to be taken seriously. The very reporting of them, in the first place, seems to me to have an element of mischief-making about it.

The Good Shepherd Seminary in Sydney, which prepares young men for the priesthood, displays a large and beautiful painting of Therry. A small card, telling future priests about the founding priest of the Mission in which they are to labour, surely takes the prize for dour negativity and downright prejudice:

> Quixotic pioneer priest, the souring agent between Polding and Bishop Willson of Hobart.

One of my early parish priests, John Joseph McGovern, was a fine pastor, but also a writer and an historian of some repute. I remember how I enjoyed listening to him holding forth on his favourite subject, but I noticed more than once that his interpretation of historical facts and my interpretation of the same facts could be quite different. The conclusions he came to from the research he shared with me would not always be the conclusions I would reach. Especially when dealing with 19th-century Irish priests or other people, I felt his understanding of their make-up and their Irishness was not fully in tune day on his endless travels, that gave power to his words and his blessings, and brought comfort, strength and love into the hearts of the countless men and women in NSW and Van Diemen's Land to whom he ministered. I feel confident about his spirituality because he imbibed from the same spiritual wells, "ever ancient, ever new", that nourish all pastors.

The only other claim that I might make is that I wear the shoes of a Cork-born person and am conscious how, for better or for worse, this can colour one's way of communicating and relating. One small example is that Therry often protested that he was "ignorant" and "lacked knowledge". In this he was taking a line out of "The Confessions of St Patrick" who protested in the same way when he heard "the call of the Irish". To make too much of this or to take it at its face value, as some have done, would be a mistake. It is a normal-enough Irish response on being offered a position of responsibility. It merely expresses an accepted degree of humility. Other than that, it has hardly any real meaning.

To use this self-confession to explain some aspects of his behaviour I find bizarre and wide of the mark. His letters alone, their logical sequence of thought and sheer volume, indicate a degree of intelligence and learning that would put him on a par with most of his professional contemporaries.

Although somewhat biased in his favour, I must confess that when I read the small print and the footnotes in the Therry literature, I had many a sinking feeling. I felt very much like throwing in the towel and leaving the pioneer priest where he is, buried in the crypt of St Mary's Cathedral — and indeed buried in the subconscious of the Church he helped to found. The main stumbling blocks for me were his antagonistic attitude towards Fr Power and other priests, his long drawn-out dispute with Bishop Willson, and his enormous land holdings. With millstones like these around his neck, how could he possibly be reinstated in the minds and hearts of contemporary people?

The one silver thread that drew me on, the light that continued to beckon over the decades, had to do with people — the ordinary people who were in the New Holland of his time. The men and women who knew him personally, or even those who heard about him first-hand, saw something in him that captivated them. As no one else before or since, he turned heads and won the hearts of what might be called the masses. "Everybody in the colonies knew that nobody could replace Therry in the peoples' affection". (Birchley, p 104)

This affection and consequent influence with Catholics and many non-Catholics worried the colonial authorities so much that when recruiting other Catholic chaplains, one criterion looked for in prospective candidates was the likelihood of their being strong enough to confront Therry's influence and break it. This same influence also worried Bishop Willson, who exclaimed in utter despair, "They have made him into a demi-god!". It has mystified and, indeed, peeved most of the modern authors; one of them put it, ". . . lay devotion to Therry continued to plague both him [Ullathorne] and Polding". (Turner, p 65)

The question I kept pondering was: "Could people, ordinary people, be so wrong?" Could the *sensus fidelium* (the consensus of ordinary believing people), which our Church once held in such high esteem, have deserted the laity of early colonial Australia? I think the very fact that, by and large, they were the poorest of the poor could, if anything, make them more clear-eyed and genuine in assessing "what was in a man" than could more comfortable and fortunate late 20th-century scholars.

This it was that drove me to re-examine the sticking points. I tried as best I could to see them from his perspective, especially his perspective as pastor and Irishman, and — lo and behold! — quite a different picture emerged. That's the picture I now present. It is the Therry story written by a non-academic for the non-academic reader.

Hesitating to describe this as biographical, I instead join Peter Robb (joint winner of the year 2000 National Biography Award for his *Life of Caravaggio*) who acknowledges that *"he had to fill in large gaps in the documentation by speculating on what might have happened"*.

I agree fully with Professor Richard Freadman, director of the unit for Studies in Biography and Autobiography at La Trobe University, who argues that

The notion of the definitive, objectively true biography is pretty much discounted now. What a biographer can do is *help you understand what is most probably true and important about a life ...* The well researched biography that admits to be dispassionate and accurate will always have its place. But now we might want the biographer to say why he was drawn to write about a particular person and *how his own life experience might help shape his view of that person.* (*Sydney Morning Herald* 22/3/2000)

I have drawn the facts for the story from the books and articles listed in the Bibliography (p 175). All references in the text are to sources listed there. I have made no specific acknowledgments except where there is a direct quote. Unidentified quotes are from Eris O'Brien's 1922 biography.

1

EARLY CLERGY —
THE CHAINED AND THE FREE

At the back of the old gaol in George Street, Sydney, a condemned convict, Paddy O'Meara, stood upon the scaffold awaiting his doom. The sheriff had delayed the execution while the priest, convinced of the man's innocence, had gone to see the Governor. The priest had often before succeeded at the last minute in overturning the verdicts of magistrates. He knew the convicts, he was their friend. He was privy to facts not mentioned in courts of law. The convicts were unfamiliar with their rights under the law. Many even had language problems, Gaelic being their first language. Virtually their only advocate was the priest, and he was often difficult to contact, being the only one in the whole of New Holland (as Australia was then called). On this particular day, he was in Parramatta giving the Last Rites to one of the survivors of the '98 Rebellion when a friend of the condemned man arrived on horseback to summon him. The priest dropped everything and headed for Sydney Town, changing horses at a farm in Bark Huts (now South Strathfield). Arriving on the scene, he begged the sheriff to stay proceedings for 15 minutes while he ran to the Governor's residence.

As time was slowly running out, the gloom around the scaffold was deepening. Although the sheriff had faith in the priest's power to obtain a reprieve, he had to do his duty. He was just about to give the nod to the executioner when the priest was seen running from the gates of Government House, waving his hat and holding up the reprieve!

Although maybe not always quite as dramatic, this kind of scene was repeated many times during Fr John Joseph Therry's early years in New South Wales. A Cork City man, born in 1790, Therry studied at St Patrick's College, Carlow, and was ordained a priest in June 1815. Even as a student, he felt drawn to missionary work and that calling became more specific through the influence of his clergy colleagues in the Cork diocese. One of them was the extraordinary and charismatic John England, ordained in Carlow a few years before Therry. Having become Bishop of Charleston, USA, at age 34, just after Therry left for Botany Bay, he was among the few Church leaders to be asked to address both houses of the US Congress, receiving a standing ovation for what critics called an inspiring and epoch-making address.

While a colleague of Therry in the Cork ministry, England had challenged the Irish Hierarchy for having, he felt, let the cause down by deciding to allow the British Government a veto on the appointment of Bishops in exchange for some material aid for the impoverished Irish Church. He forced the Bishops to think again and eventually to abandon the idea because of the people-power he was able to muster.

Actively involved in that campaign was one Richard Hayes OFM, officially based in Rome. His brother Michael, a ticket-of-leave man in NSW, made fervent pleas to Richard to use his influence to secure some Irish priests to minister to the convicts "down under". John England's interest in convicts and especially the appalling conditions of those being transported to NSW, was aired in the pages of the influential *Cork Mercantile Review*, of which he was a Board member.

> The prisoners were so tightly crowded on board the convict ships that they were each allowed only 18 inches of space on which to lie ... of the ten men who died on the *Britannia*, six were the result of floggings, while two others who had been flogged died from drinking their own urine when refused their water ration. Many of the women convicts were

publicly beaten ... or had their heads shaved. Others were placed in irons, chained or placed in the neck-yoke. (Costello)

So successfully did John England challenge the greatest power in the land that Undersecretary Goulburn, who was in charge of transportation, was forced to take the rather drastic step of setting up a Royal Commission, which ultimately led to better conditions.

John England's influence on Therry will become more obvious as the latter's amazing feeling for convicts and his courage in challenging authority figures, both civil and ecclesiastical, on what, to his mind, were matters of justice, is described.

Education was another area in which England seems to have influenced the young Therry. Very much aware that schools were widely used for proselytising purposes, England spearheaded a campaign to set up schools according to the Lancaster System — schools, that is, that were open to the poor and were non-sectarian: if Catholic parents, for instance, wanted their children instructed in their own faith, they would need to send them to school one hour early. England opened the first of these schools, the Mardyke school in Cork. He not only taught in it, but he produced most of the textbooks. Therry was to face an almost identical situation in New Holland and later in Van Diemen's Land. His response remarkably paralleled England's.

Probably because of the pleas of Richard Hayes OFM and the sad stories emanating from his younger brother Thomas England (ordained the same year as Terry) and chaplain to Cork gaol, John England is said to have volunteered for Botany Bay himself and to have likewise encouraged a Fr Jeremiah O'Flynn. O'Flynn, unfortunately, set sail in 1817 without proper Home Office or ecclesiastical approval. Governor Lachlan Macquarie refused to accept him in Sydney and even had him banished from the colony. His expulsion, picked up by the English and Irish media, was such an embarrassment to the British Government that the

appointment of an official Catholic chaplain to Botany
Bay became a matter of urgency.

For Therry and England, O'Flynn painted a grand
picture of thousands of convicts in Botany Bay eagerly
awaiting the day when they would have a priest of their
own. This was an overly optimistic perception of the
priorities of the penal colony's inhabitants. He is still
remembered, however, as the one said to have reserved
the Blessed Sacrament in the house of James Dempsey or
William Davis in Kent Street at the last Mass he celebrated
in Sydney Town. Governor Macquarie sent him back on
the same ship on which he came:

> Being well persuaded he would do a great deal of
> mischief among the lower order of Catholics ...
> whose religious feelings might be worked upon by a
> designing artful priest so as to excite a spirit of
> resistance, insubordination, insurrection ... (Kiernan,
> p 35)

O'Flynn would have apprised Therry of the three other
priests, James Harold, Peter O'Neill and James Dixon, who
had preceded him to NSW. They were convicts
transported because of some perceived complicity in the
'98 Rebellion. Father Harold, who arrived on the *Minerva*
in January 1800, was in the colony less than 12 months
when he was sentenced to imprisonment on Norfolk
Island for unproven involvement in the Parramatta
uprising of that year. In reference to this Eris O'Brien
remarks:

> Governor   King   panicked,   officials   became
> melodramatic and magistrates berserk, at rumours of
> conspiracy rather than facts of insurrection .... but as
> an   instance   of   brutality   in   punishment,   it   is
> unsurpassed in our history. (1953)

Although a committee of officers found that "no act or
fact" relative to a conspiracy had been clearly established,
five suspects were given 1,000 lashes each, four 500, seven
200, and all were transported out of New South Wales.
Before being banished to Norfolk Island with them,
Fr Harold, as a mark of infamy, was forced to place his

hands around the whipping tree while certain of the prisoners were being scourged. He remained in Norfolk as a convict, exercising his teaching skills and (in secret) his ministry, till 1807, when he was sent to Van Diemen's Land. In 1809, on being given a conditional pardon, he sailed to the USA and thence to Ireland, in 1815.

The only one allowed to minister publicly in a limited way was James Dixon, who also arrived in the year 1800. He had been charged with commanding a company of rebels in a town in County Wexford — where he had never been! Even the Protestant clergy and prominent citizens of the district had gone to the trouble of protesting to the Lord Lieutenant of Ireland that the priest was innocent.

His voyage on the *Friendship* with 134 convicts, 19 of whom died en route, was quite horrendous. One convict later wrote home: "Fr Dixon during his journey out on a boat that took six months to do the trip was chained to a dead corpse until the rats ate the flesh off the bones of the corpse." (Costello)

In New South Wales, Dixon managed to win the confidence of Governor Philip Gidley King to such an extent that in 1801 King even petitioned the Home Office for a free pardon for all three priests.

In his response in 1802, Lord Hobart refused the pardon, but surprised King by suggesting that they be allowed to pursue their clerical functions with compensation! When making the formal proclamation in 1803, allowing Dixon only to celebrate Mass, King stated, in the grandiloquent language of the day, that the concession to Catholics proceeded from "the benevolence and piety of our Most Gracious Majesty". The irony is, of course, that the Gracious Majesty in question, George III, was anything but gracious to Catholics. He was, in fact, notoriously anti-Catholic, and as O'Brien astutely remarks, "of all the men, at that time in England, George III would be the last to make such a concession deliberately!". Lord Hobart is the one to be thanked and, to some extent, Governor King, who implemented the ministerial recommendation.

Thus on May 15th 1803, 15 years after the foundation of the colony, Mass was celebrated publicly for the first time. Weekly Mass in Sydney Town and Parramatta and the Hawkesbury became the norm for almost 12 months, until the Castle Hill Rising in March 1804. King, who had always had misgivings about Irish gatherings, was convinced that the Masses in Parramatta must have been used to do some underground planning.

Although King was unable to implicate Dixon in any way with the Rising, "like Harold a few years earlier, Dixon was severely humiliated in that while 30 men were being flogged in his presence, he was forced to place his hands on their bleeding backs, as a result of which he swooned and had to be removed". (Cardinal Moran, quoted by O'Brien 1953.) The public celebration of Mass being forbidden (not to be resumed for another 15 years), Dixon returned to Ireland in 1808. Manning Clark's comments seem to have some relevance:

> ... members of the Protestant ascendance of NSW never paused to sort out the muddle in their own minds on the origins of revolts, blaming indiscriminately the Irish, the priests, the Church of Rome, the ideas of "1798". (Vol 1, p 173)

A person of "the most notorious seditious and rebellious principles" was how Peter O'Neill, parish priest of Ballymacoda, County Cork, was described. He was actually anti-revolutionary but, refusing to inform on his parishioners involved in the '98 Rebellion, he was given 275 lashes and transported, untried, with 137 other "desperate and diabolical characters" on the *Luz St Ann* in 1801.

When the Lord Lieutenant realised that a mistake had been made, he ordered O'Neill's immediate release. By then, however, King had sentenced him to penal servitude in Norfolk Island, and it was nearly three years before he got back to East Cork. By now the number of United Irishmen in the colony was rising rapidly, and the colonial authorities, becoming quite nervous, asked the Home Government to cool rebel transportation for a while.

Even before the departure of the First Fleet, Irish priests or priests of Irish descent had been in touch with the prisoners and had requested permission to accompany those who were to be transported. The 1787 colonial papers (Public Record Office, London) include a letter to Lord Sydney from "Thomas Walshe, priest", applying for permission for himself and another priest to go to Botany Bay with the convicts:

> I do not think I can ever be as happy as in the place of their destination ... we are not so presumptuous as to wish support from the Government. We offer our voluntary services. We hope, however, not to offend in entreaty for our passage. (O'Brien 1953)

There is another undated document among the 1791 colonial papers at the Public Record Office in London, stating that "for many years three Roman Catholic priests attend to the Roman Catholic convicts on board the hulks at Woolwich and Gosport ... and Newgate ... the number of those transported to Botany Bay is about 800". Evidently these priests, too, had volunteered, promising that "the most moderate terms the Government would think proper to prescribe, they would readily accept".

The fact that priests were knocking on the door of officialdom requesting "the privilege" of being allowed to accompany men and women condemned to penal servitude and banished to the ends of the earth, is inspiring indeed. The fact that officialdom seems to have made no effort to open doors to them is equally disillusioning.

Six days after Captain Phillip brought the First Fleet into Botany Bay, on January 26th 1788, two priests arrived on board two French discovery ships. They were acting as scientists. One of them, named Receveur, was ill on arrival and died on February 17th 1788. He was buried just inside North Head in La Perouse, a couple of weeks before the ships departed.

A Spanish priest arrived at Sydney Cove in March 1793 as chaplain to a Spanish ship on a voyage of discovery. On learning that no Church building of any kind had yet been constructed, he is reported to have remarked that "had the place been settled by his nation, a house of God would have been erected before any house of man". Perhaps this remark was related to the Anglican chaplain, the Rev Mr Johnson, because a wattle and daub church was opened a few months later — the very first in the penal colony.

2

MISSION IMPOSSIBLE

The catalyst for Therry came as he was doing an errand in the city while acting as secretary to the Bishop of Cork. Crossing Patrick's Street, he noticed people's attention being drawn to a group of British soldiers leading several horse-drawn drays in which were herded a large number of men in chains. He learned they were his fellow countrymen on their way to Queenstown, where they would await transportation to the penal colony of Botany Bay. A few of them, he was told, were the last of the surviving '98 men. Therry, feeling deeply for them, rushed into the nearest store and bought up all the medals and prayerbooks he could find. These he threw to the men, with the promise that he himself would follow them to the far-away Antipodes.

As he walked away, the vacant fearful eyes of these men haunted him. The feeling at the time was that transportation was a fate worse than death. At his Mass for the nurses at the North Infirmary that morning, he had said some words about a woman in the Gospel whom Jesus cured. (Luke 13:10ff) She is referred to as being "held bound", "bent double", "enfeebled", "unable to stand upright". Therry had explained to the nurses that she can be taken as a symbol of the wounded ones to whom Jesus ministered. He had pointed out that her problem wasn't just the infirmity she was suffering, but the low standing she had in people's eyes. She was thought to be more in the possession of Satan than of God, and that, in such a religious society, meant that she was looked down on, despised, excluded.

Jesus, however, noticed her, called her over and laid his hand on her. As he did, she looked into his eyes and saw the love there. In those eyes she was good and beautiful and important, and suddenly for the first time in 18 years, she stood up straight. Therry had reminded the nurses that they were called to bring that compassion of Jesus to people who were "held bound", "enfeebled", "unable to stand upright".

Now, as he walked back to the Bishop's house, he realised that his calling in life was to bring that same healing love of Jesus not to the people in his native city, but to those forlorn men in the drays, even if it meant following them to the ends of the earth.

The thought of leaving his family and friends forever and heading off on a gruelling six-month voyage into the unknown was a daunting one. But once he had made up his mind that this was his vocation, nothing would stop him.

Remarkably, he didn't have to wait long. The British Government, concluding that the only way to deal with Irish prisoners in Botany Bay was through a minister of their own religion, called for a show of interest. John Joseph Therry responded forthwith, as did Philip Conolly, who was some years his senior.

Arriving in Sydney on May 3rd 1820, on board the ship *Janus*, Fr Therry was hardly ever again to be free of trauma of one kind or another. He was 33 years old. As contemporary Anglican James Bonisch remembers him:

> He possessed a spirit of independence and boldness of expression. Very small in stature, slight in figure but wiry in frame, active in mind and body, he had beneath the sacerdotal robe the soul of a revolutionist ... yet with all his fiery zeal and reputed turbulence he was of a really lovable nature, with the very simplicity of a child. (p 123)

Even the six-month voyage from Queenstown, now Cobh, in Cork Harbour, via Rio de Janeiro to Sydney became the subject of an inquiry. On board were 105 young women prisoners with 26 children, huddled together in the most squalid and primitive conditions. Many of them, in their desperation and will to survive, accepted gifts from the ship's crew in return for sexual favours. At the inquiry Fr Therry and his companion, Fr Conolly, gave evidence that was very critical of the ship's officers, as well as of the sailors and, indeed, of the whole convict transportation arrangements.

The Governor of the day, Lachlan Macquarie, received the two officially appointed chaplains with some misgivings — not that he was anti-Catholic, he was just unaccustomed to dealing with clergy of other Churches. In his experience, wherever the British flag was unfurled, there, by that very fact, the Protestant Church became the national and established religion. He found that to his liking. It made it simpler and easier for him to govern and control the new colony.

After giving a lot of thought to the new situation, Macquarie received Therry and Conolly graciously, but he gave them a document of rules and regulations that made ministry almost impossible for a man like Therry, who combined strength of character with a total commitment to justice and fair play. Among the sticking points were:

- a total prohibition on receiving a non-Catholic into the Catholic Church;
- a prohibition on ministering in any way to sick or dying non-Catholics;
- a total prohibition on marrying a Catholic and a non-Catholic; and
- a total prohibition on visiting or having any presence at the Orphan School.

Even the marriage of two Catholics could only be undertaken after all sorts of bureaucratic time-consuming permissions were obtained. This system might work in tranquil settled times, but it was utterly unreasonable in the hurly-burly of a penal colony pushing its frontiers into the New South Wales hinterland and slowly and painfully developing some semblance of civilised living.

Macquarie saw this expression of his power and control as necessary for the good order of the colony.

rivers, here called creeks, amazed him. As he passed through to some distant outpost, they were mostly flat dry clay beds but, when he returned some days later they could be almost impassable, so full had they become.

He became aware, too, of the emptiness and loneliness. In his home country, there was a family abode every couple of hundred metres. In this new land of such immense distances and bare horizons, he could travel all day without seeing even a hut.

What intrigued him most of all were the animals, especially the ones who carried their young in pouches, the marsupials. Preaching and teaching being very much part of his liturgical services, he peppered his homilies with references to the variety of kangaroos, wallabies, possums and koalas he encountered on his way to Parramatta or Liverpool or wherever. The birds, too, were a fascination to him and to his congregations: the crimson rosella and the king parrot lighting up the bush with jewel-bright colours; the laughing kookaburras greeting the dawn from some high perches; the cockatoos, with their beautiful crest of feathers, accompanying him with screeches and squawks, initially frightening his horse, but making the long hours on the track so much more interesting.

As a priest, Therry was obliged to spend considerable time each day (at least 90 minutes) reading or reciting "The Office of the Hours", so called because its different sections corresponded to the different hours or stages of the day. Made up mostly of the psalms, the office was a duty of love for Therry, one he never missed, no matter how busy he was or how far he had to travel. In fact, he found that the psalms gave a new dimension to the distant travelling. He could chant them on the saddle or resting in some cool shade. They lifted his spirits and gave expression to an other-worldly aspect of his new experiences.

Therry's Celtic spirituality was akin to that of the Aborigines in that it integrated the natural and the supernatural, creation and the Creator. The Book of Job reflected this awareness of the divine in things. He liked to quote:

> If you would learn more ask the cattle [or the Kangaroos]
> Seek information from the birds of the air.
> There is not one such creature but will know this state of things is all of God's own making.
> He holds in his power every living thing ... (12:7–9)

Life in colonial NSW was indeed daunting and sometimes troubling but, for a man of faith, it was also exciting and very satisfying.

3

THE CRY OF THE POOR

On a wintry day in 1823, Fr Therry found himself on the southern banks of the Hawkesbury near Penrith, unable to cross the swollen river. He was on his way to give the Last Rites to a prisoner who was about to be hanged at Emu Plains. Convicts went to great pains to contact him at times like these. In notes written in a primitive scrawly hand and surreptitiously delivered, they would plead with him "by all that's holy" to come. Therry's presence at all times, but especially at times of crisis, seemed to be crucial to them. They would take any risk to get word to him. And he always responded, no matter what the distance or the weather or state of the track (if any). As so often happened, he was now in a very frustrating predicament; neither horse nor boat could brave the fast-flowing current.

What to do? Seeing some people on the other side, he shouted to them for help in God's name and in the name of a dying convict. Imaginatively enough, they procured a rope which, with the aid of a stone, they were able to throw across the river to him. Therry tied the rope around his body, jumped into the river and was dragged through the dangerous passage by the people on the other side. Without stopping evidently for a rest or a change of clothes, he mounted another horse and arrived in time to bring the consolation of religion to the condemned prisoner.

Therry spent the greater part of each day in the saddle. A horse was always ready and harnessed at the front gate. On returning from a distant call, the tired horse was given a rest, the harnessed one taken and a second harnessed horse readied in case of emergencies. Distances held no terror for him. He said Mass twice every Sunday, once in Sydney Town and the other 25 km away, either in Parramatta or Liverpool, at least a two-hour trek each way on a good horse. Mass was always followed by religious instructions for children and adults. To visit gaols, hospitals, road gangs and dying convicts, he covered a radius of over 300 km.

Overnight he stayed in homes which were often slab huts made from sheets of stringy bark and hessian. The beds were bunks formed by sheets of bark placed on trestles and covered with sacks of straw — often the abode of lice and fleas.

The windows, without glass, attracted fresh clean air but also in summer mosquitoes and other vermin, which made sleeping very difficult and sometimes impossible. Lighting was by slush lamp or evil-smelling candle made of mutton fat.

A leaf from Therry's diary indicates an amazing degree of stamina and enthusiasm, especially when it's remembered that the saddle doesn't afford any protection from the heat and humidity of summer and the bitter southerlies of winter. A typical entry is as follows: On Tuesday, he travelled from Sydney to Parramatta and thence to Seven Hills, where he stayed overnight at Kelly's (approx 40 km). Wednesday he wound his way a further 20 km to Windsor, where three men were under sentence of death. Thursday, on to Richmond for the marriage of John Donovan and Mary Nowlan. Friday was really hectic: he rushed back to Windsor, where a young man had died overnight and six men under sentence of death needed him. He visited a dear old man called Lawler, living in a *skilling* who wanted to confess. In the late afternoon, he headed for Parramatta and thence to Sydney, arriving God knows when. Saturday he did lots of calls in Sydney, and on Sunday, it was on to Parramatta for Mass, after which he was urgently called back to Sydney ...

Even in an air-conditioned car and on four-lane highways, the clergyman of today would have difficulty keeping up with a schedule like this! One has to keep in mind that the tracks were wheelruts made by drays pulled generally by teams of bullocks, led by a bullocky (himself often an ex-convict). In heavy rain, in the low-lying spots, the track became a quagmire, which even Therry's horse would find hard to negotiate. Often marooned drays would remain immobile for days, even weeks, waiting for the sun and wind to firm up the clay once more. Sometimes Therry found it necessary to make detours involving many extra hours in the saddle. When the workload couldn't be completed in the daylight hours, it was not uncommon for him to spend the night in the saddle between Sydney, Parramatta, Liverpool, Windsor, Emu Plains, etc . . .

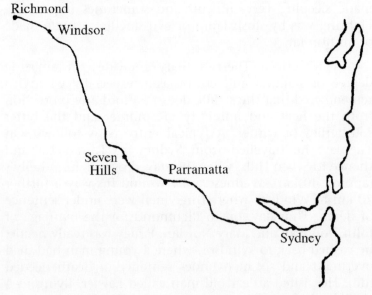

Crossing rivers at a time when bridges were non-existent or few and far between was a hazardous operation. The first fordable crossing, for example, of the Cook's River, which flows into Botany Bay from the southwest, was at Bark Huts, so called because a number of shanties, made of bark, had been erected there. Said to be a day's walk or a day's dray ride from Sydney Town, it was a convenient overnight stop en route to the Illawarra or to Liverpool or even Parramatta. It grew into quite a settlement eventually, with its own small goods store and even a tannery business. Having a spare horse awaiting him there gave Therry greater travel capacity. His dream of building something came closer to reaslisation when he was given a small parcel of land there in the 1830s but the actual building didn't come until some years later.

On a visit to the gaol at Emu Plains (80 km west of Sydney at the foot of the Blue Mountains), Therry met a minister called Dr Halloran, with whom he became good friends. Although they only met more or less by accident while attending to their respective convict flocks, they liked to discuss the problem of finding God in a penal colony, where just about everyone was deemed either law-breaker or law enforcer. Finding Jesus in such an unlikely environment posed somewhat of a problem. In Therry's homeland, faith was in the atmosphere, in the very air people breathed. The post-Penal Laws' freedom unlocked churches and brought into the open a wide variety of religious practices. Here it was so different.

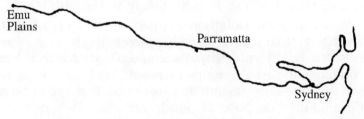

Halloran shared with Therry an extract from St Luke's Gospel that he had just used in his gaol service. In it Jesus says to two of the disciples of John the Baptist (in gaol at the time) "... Go and tell John what you see and hear". (7:22) They went and told John that Jesus was with the poor, the sick, the lame, the blind, prisoners, prostitutes and sinners ... The people who were behind the eight ball, the failures, the nobodies and the excluded were being healed and ministered to and raised up. When

John heard this, he gave a great cry of delight and praise. Great prophet that he was, he knew that was exactly where the Anointed One, the Saviour, should be.

Therry and his companion knew, too, that this was the answer to their problem. Therry had experienced that divine something in the faces he saw even in the dark foreboding prison cells, the chain gangs, the scaffold, the tread-mill ... Sometimes he got glimpses of the thorn-crowned Head, the pillar dripping with blood from the scourged back, the Crucified breathing forth his soul ... Many a time, he had seen dense threatening clouds move rapidly to the north, revealing the bright reassuring outline of the Southern Cross over the blue waters of Botany Bay. The strong mystic streak in him knew that in the most unlikely of places, where hearts and bodies were being bruised and battered, the hidden light and the silent music can be detected by eyes and ears that are in tune. This motivated him. It assured him that, in the incessant travelling, he was being guided by the star that, even in the Antipodes, leads to hidden treasure.

The Kellys at Seven Hills gave Therry great hope. Kelly was one of a small number of former convicts who were beginning to get on their feet by the 1820s. Some among them had a strong attachment to the faith.

According to Columbus Fitzpatrick, who was a boy in Sydney at that time, Church activity (such as it was) between Fr O'Flynn's departure and Therry's arrival was conducted by small groups of people here and there, in some faint way resembling, perhaps, the present-day Communitas de Base of South America. This memory etched in the mind of an old man looking back 40 years would seem to indicate that the laity had somewhat more of a role in the origins of the Australian Church than they have normally been given credit for.

> After the departure of Fr O'Flynn, the Catholics in the different parts of the colony formed themselves into committees, having for their centres Mr Lacey of Parramatta, Mr Dwyer of Liverpool, Mr Byrne of Campbelltown, Mr Kenny of Appin etc so that there

was a union in prayer and an intercourse of intelligence among all classes of Catholics in the country ... (Turner p 39)

As Ed Campion points out:

Catholic convicts brought their faith with them and kept it alive, however fitfully, throughout the succeeding years. Almost uniquely in world history Catholicism in Australia was founded not by Bishops or priests ... but by the laity — and convict laity at that. Here is truly a Church of Sinners. Here, right from the start, the saint and larrikin can be found in the one person! (p 3)

4

"THE FELON'S FRIEND"

The great tree in the square at Campbelltown provided shelter from the sun and the elements for many a gathering in the 1820s. It was where people gathered on Sunday mornings for Fr Therry's Mass. He would already have celebrated Mass in Liverpool, or even in Sydney, before mounting his newly acquired two-wheel gig for the long trek south. Saying Mass in the open after hours of dusty travel in all kinds of weather was not a great problem for the rugged pioneer. The fasting from midnight, even in sweltering summer conditions, he regarded as par for the course.

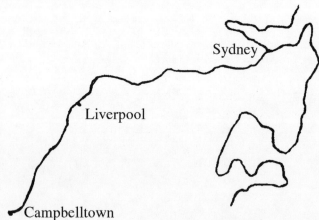

One of the many stories passed down about those late Sunday morning Masses in Campbelltown in the early 1820s had to do with the weather. The convicts and others had gathered under the great tree. They had come from Appin and Menangle and even as far south as

Berrima. Therry was about to move to the rickety altar-
table when a dark menacing cloud began to emit large
drops of sleet and water. They knew the tree would be no
match for the gathering storm. What to do? Someone
pointed to an almost completed Anglican Church
building just across the way. They looked at the priest,
already in his vestments. Therry didn't wait: "Go for it!"
he indicated and thus the first religious service in the
Campbelltown Anglican Church was a Catholic Mass!

The Rector, Rev Mr Reddall (the local magistrate),
was very angry, feeling his beautiful new church had been
desecrated. He demanded an explanation. The reply was
vintage Therry: "I have the same respect for you that I
had prior to receiving your letter; your being a magistrate
has no terrors for me. It is not unusual for your Church
and mine to hold divine service in the same building ...
my Church is more restrictive in discipline than yours, yet
it permits such usage. I took the liberty in question,
anticipating your consent ..."

There were no apologies or beg pardons. In Therry's
estimation the Rev Mr Reddall should have felt honoured,
rather than chagrined! Given the perception of heresy by
both Communities regarding each other, and the
consequent tension and sometimes bitterness, Therry's
action was courageous, indeed.

Strictly speaking what he did was wrong and could
have been a source of scandal for his own flock. However
it showed a high degree of common sense and
commendable freedom from legalism.

To give him his due, the Rev Reddall must have had
second thoughts because, some years later, when Therry
was building St John's Church in Campbelltown, Reddall
made a generous donation to him.

Some escaped convicts (from road gangs and gaols),
who became the bushrangers and outlaws of the day,
once intercepted Therry on one of his many expeditions
south of Campbelltown. As soon as his identity was
discovered, they released him at once, with expressions of
regret for delaying him. Subsequently, in his journeying

over rough bridle trails through ranges and forests, it became a bushy tradition that he was never to be molested, but treated with courtesy and respect and helped on his way. Primitive though it was, the Bush Telegraph carried far and wide his reputation as "the friend of the convicts" (when they had precious few friends). He was known as the one person who loved them with an intense devoted love, and even the fiercest and worst of them soon began to return his affection.

Between 1795 and 1841, 24,789 Irish convicts arrived in Australia. Some were political prisoners involved in the insurrection of 1798 and many of these, Therry noticed, were among his leading supporters — men like James Meehan, William Davis, James Dempsey, Hugh Byrne and others, including many Protestants. The '98 Rebellion was the brainchild of the United Irishmen, a movement initiated by Theobold Wolfe Tone and fellow Presbyterians in Belfast in 1791. Strange to say, this movement, as the name suggests, had ecumenical overtones in that it sought to unite the Catholics in the South and the Protestants in the North in the cause of Irish freedom. It recognised that the real demarcation in people's lives was not Protestant/Catholic but superior race/inferior race, oppressor/oppressed. All other divisions, including the religious one, were deliberately fomented to distract people from the really important issues which the poor and oppressed in the North and the South held in common. The great overriding social sin was imperialism; private sin paled into insignificance before it.

In 1798 tens of thousands of United Irishmen, Protestant and Catholic, gave their lives in a desperate attempt to draw world attention to this problem. Many of the survivors, perhaps up to one thousand, were summarily transported to Botany Bay without trial or formal sentence. Such was the dread of transportation that many of them begged to be hanged, rather than face the dark unknown. This dread was deliberately fostered, so that transportation, seen as the ultimate punishment, would be a powerful deterrent to insubordination and crime. As bushranger Ben Hall put it:

You'll have no chance for mischief then —
Remember what I say,
They'll flog mischief out of you
When you get to Botany Bay.
The waves were high upon the sea,
The winds blew up in gales;
I'd rather be drowned in misery
Than go to New South Wales. (Clune, p 53)

Colonial Secretary Bathurst wrote to Governor Thomas Brisbane in Sydney on September 9th 1822, warning against any form of mitigation and enjoining him "to restore to their original character the terrors of transportation":

... the strict discipline, the unremitting labour, the severe but wholesome privations, the estrangements from the sweets and comforts of life ... (HRAX 7)

And of course the ever-ready "cat" must be insisted on at all times and in all circumstances. Father John McEncroe, who was to become Therry's best friend, witnessed the cat being used on a man who talked back to a supervisor. Years later he recalled:

The cat (photo section, p 3), with hardwood handle, nine thongs plaited and knotted every few inches, is whirled around the head of the flogger; the cruel lash descends. The blows are all delivered on the same spot. Blue streaks are imprinted on the quivering flesh by the first lash. Those gradually change their line to black, and finally to red, when the blood begins to trickle down the body. The mate of the unfortunate man — a lad of 18 or 19 years of age — stands by weeping bitterly, but powerless to offer help. How is it with the sufferer himself? He twice repeats the words "hit fair" as the thongs overreach themselves and twist themselves round his body — with this exception, he betrays no sign of the terrible agony he is enduring. (Birchley, p 43)

O'Brien (1953) quotes the *Memoirs* of Holt, describing how:

> Paddy Galvin, a young lad of 20, suspected, in 1800, of being involved in planning a rising, received his first 100 lashes on his shoulders until the shoulder blades were bared; the next 100 on his buttocks and finally on his calves, until the flesh in each place was reduced to pulp.

This was the punishment of an *unconvicted* man, merely to extort evidence! Rev Samuel Marsden, a leading magistrate, testifies to Governor King in a similar and contemporary case:

> The prisoner was examined again yesterday. He behaved so very insolently that Mr Atkins and I ordered him to be punished very severely in hopes of making him inform where the pikes were. Tho' a young man he would have died on the spot before he would tell a single sentence. He was taken down three times — punished on the back and also on his bottom when he could receive no more on his back. He was just in the same mood when taken to hospital as when first tied up, and continues the same this morning ... I am sure he will die before he will reveal anything of this business. (O'Brien, 1953)

Birchley adds:

> When one recalls that the victims of these scourges walked away with the blood from their backs squelching in their shoes and that fifty lashes was the penalty for failing to lift the hat to a passing Magistrate, the horror becomes manifest. (pp 43–44)

The flogging in Norfold Island of Maurice Fitzgerald from Cork is described by an eye witness:

> The first blow made the blood spout out of Fitzgerald's shoulders, and I felt so disgusted and horrified that I turned away ... One of the constables forced me *to look at my peril*. The day was windy, and although I was 15 yards to leeward from the sufferer, the blood, skin and flesh blew in my face as the executioners shook it off their cats. (Costello)

As E A Martin writes: The colony maintained a brutal convict system based on the cat-o-nine tails, the chain gang and the treadmill. Between 1830 and 1837 nearly two million lashes were inflicted on the 32,102 convicts in New South Wales. (p 2)

A famous author who embraced Christianity, Simone Weil, wrote perceptively in 1938 that the two forms of punishment which filled her with most abhorrence were solitary confinement and confinement in a penal colony, and she screamed out in protest to the French Government to abandon both ... They are inseparable from servitude and oppression. (Kennedy) Although some Irish and English convicts were criminals of the worst type, most were guilty of rather minor offences, like stealing a bag of oats, a fowl, a sheep, or some other such. No matter how young the offender might be or how trivial the crime, he was billeted with the others and treated as if he were a hardened criminal.

To respond to the increasing number of urgent calls coming from the widely scattered convicts, Therry testifies that he "frequently had been obliged to procure three or four horses in the course of the day". Often the calls were from Protestants condemned to death and wishing to die in the Catholic faith. Letters, passed on through tradesmen or indulgent warders, breathe an atmosphere of trust and appreciation for this man, who gave his whole heart to their welfare:

> Sam Chipp under sentence of death for murder of black native, do not know when death warrants will arrive ... for God's sake do not delay to come for I am resolved to die a Catholic when you come ... do not delay ... Joe Lockett ordered for execution next Monday wishes to die a Catholic ... Young man in sells [sic] sadly troubled wishes to see you very particular for he burst into tears last night and cried out for your assistance ... The low ebb of misery and degradation to which John Wall is reduced [of which Therry had had much experience] urges him to trespass on the priest's well-known goodness ...

Webb who is under sentence of execution and who
has been brought up in the Protestant religion
earnestly solicits your attendance to give him an
opportunity of confessing and dying in the Catholic
faith ... The following ("including a female: Brigid
Fairless") have had sentence of death passed on them
this day wishes your attendance at your earliest
opportunity ...

When attending people condemned to death Therry,
with great effect, used the story from Luke about the two
thieves who were crucified on crosses beside Jesus on
Calvary's hill. One is called the good thief, but Therry
didn't think the other one was that bad, either. This latter
said to Jesus, "Look, if you're the Messiah, you can save us
from these wretched crosses and this wretched death".
Like any of us, he was preoccupied with the here and
now. The other man, in Therry's eyes, had the far-seeing
eye, he had the big vision. Even on the crucible of the
cross, he could see beyond the horizons of this world and,
amazingly, in the dying powerless agonising man next to
him, he could feel the aura of the divine. He raised
himself so as to get the words out: "Jesus, remember me
when you come into your Kingdom". The response Therry
repeated with feeling and deep empathy for the man
facing the scaffold: "This very day you will be with me in
paradise".

These words resonated deeply with Therry himself.
Seeing this, the prisoner's heart was invariably moved and
comforted. Numerous letters addressed to Therry from
gaols attest to the amazing success of his ministry. The
secret of his attraction was that these people saw no
superiority or holier-than-thou attitude reflected in his
dealings with them. They felt at home with him; his were
wounded hands and feet like theirs. He was deeply
impressed by the fact that Jesus broke all the canons of
social and religious correctness by being friend to tax
collectors and sinners, to those who were excluded from
the mailing lists of respectable people.

5

"THE LAMBS ARE ABROAD ..."

There was one government institution in Sydney that was totally off limits to Therry from the beginning. It was one of Governor Macquarie's no-go areas. Its closure to him was a running sore that annoyed and frustrated him, day in day out. Like St Paul with his "thorn in the flesh", he beseeched the Lord and the authorities, in season and out of season, to have the ban lifted, but to no avail. The institution in question was the Sydney Orphan School. It was the only one of its kind in the early 1820s, more were opened later.

The school was indicative of the state of morality at the time, which was said to be at a low ebb in all sectors of society. The school wasn't restricted to orphans in the strict sense. Some children there had parents who couldn't or wouldn't provide for them. Many were children of convict fathers; many, too, had been born out of wedlock to women in the Female Factory. Some had been born to convict mothers who were forced to go back to work as soon as their children were weaned. The parents of some had received a second sentence or had their ticket of leave cancelled. Some of the children had come with their mothers from overseas, but their convict fathers, being still in servitude, couldn't maintain them. And of course there were the usual tragic casualties of sickness and misfortune, which affected both free and bound.

The Orphan School was run by the Government with a proviso that only the Protestant religion would be taught. Catholic children were welcomed, provided they changed their religion and, once they enrolled, they could not be withdrawn. Since Catholics were about one third of the population of the colony at that time, that would likely be the proportion of Catholic children at the school.

Manning Clark puts the case thus:

> Therry campaigned against the partial, impolite and unjust system of forcing children in the orphan school whose parents were Catholic to receive religious instruction from the Protestant Chaplains. He asked the Government to allow these children to be instructed in the rites of their own religion and to be exempted from conforming to Protestant forms of worship. He implored the Colonial Secretary to conceive of the situation of a parent about to depart this life whose children must go into an orphanage and so sacrifice a religion which the dying parent cherished as something far more precious than property or even than life. Surely their plight was worth a sympathetic ear. (p 32)

Therry knew of similar institutions, called "charter schools", set up in Ireland. They operated for some time but, once their true intent was discovered, such was the adverse reaction that the British Government was forced to close them down. Since the Orphan Schools were the only hope Catholic children had of getting an education, relatives were constantly appealing to Therry to do something. He tried every possible means he could think of to prise open the doors so that at least some form of Catholic scripture could be offered to the Catholic children there, but to no avail. In desperation he opened a small Catholic school in Parramatta and one in Sydney in 1822, but finance was the big problem, and neither school lasted very long.

The language of his letters to Macquarie and his successors was sometimes gentle and persuasive, at other times strong and urgent. The tone of his continuing pleas may be seen in a letter to the Colonial Secretary: "The lambs are abroad ... must the Watchman hold his peace?

Is he to be silent? Is he to be worse than a dumb dog? Is he, by consulting his personal interests or his personal safety, to betray his precious trust, purchased as it has been by his Divine Master's most precious blood?" (1826)

This kind of language irritated colonial officialdom no end, especially the then Governor, Ralph Darling, who was unsympathetic to Therry and his cause in any case.

He couldn't stand the gentle irony of Therry's letters. He found them "offensive", "insulting", "full of improper observations and invectives". In fact, Therry's language almost verged on flattery. To soften whatever complaints or criticisms he wanted to make, his words, in the discursive style of the day, were nuanced in all sorts of ways and were not at all as harsh as claimed. To say as, T Southerwood does, that "he boldly and bluntly attacked the authorities" would seem to be overstating it. When angry perhaps he did speak from the shoulder and tell it as he saw it, but that doesn't seem to have been his normal style (at least his writing style).

To the Governor he was an enigma, a man who wouldn't give up or give in:

Overlooking utilitarian reasons or party interests he asked whether a law or regulation was morally justifiable! Threats were of no avail when he perceived a moral issue.

Indeed Therry himself admitted that he would not abandon a single essential principle of his religion to please the King or his representative, much as he would make any sacrifice to serve, please and gratify both! Writing to the Home Office Darling described him as "a man of strong feelings ... disposed to be troublesome, even dangerous ... I have no desire to see any more clergy of Catholic persuasion here ...". He suggested that if, in future, another Catholic priest were sent out, an Englishman should have preference, adding somewhat ironically, "All the Catholics here are Irish!".

Although Darling's predecessor, Governor Brisbane, cited Therry approvingly as a model for Presbyterian ministers to follow, in order to strengthen his appeal to

London to send out more priests, he claimed all major crimes committed since he arrived were attributable to Catholics,

> who were so bereft of every advantage that could adorn the mind of man that soon there would be nothing but the shade of their skin to distinguish them from the Aborigines. He had hoped they would dwindle away or become engrafted with the Protestants but as they seemed to cherish their faith as dearly as their lives and as their priest [Therry] counselled obedience and subordination with the same zeal as the Protestant Chaplains he had agreed reluctantly to contribute to the building of a Chapel for them. (Manning Clark, p 83)

Today, when it is stated that most crime committed in Australia is attributable to Asians, hard statistics can be used in its refutation. No such precise statistics existed in the early 1820s. Brisbane's feeling was probably in tune with the general feeling that Catholics (the underdogs) were to blame for everything.

As O'Farrell puts it:

> Hostility to Catholicism was built into the structures and assumptions of colonial society. The accepted image of the Irish Catholic was that of an obnoxious dangerous inferior, an image that normally provoked hostility and suspicion among those so depicted. (p 54)

(This is something Catholics of Irish ethnic origin should remember when confronted with anti-Asian rhetoric today.)

In the mid 1820s Mrs Darling, the Governor's wife, gave some hope by opening a "School of Industry". Therry alerted Catholics that this might be an opportunity for their children, only to be told on opening day that the Governor's rule applied: only Protestants or those willing to become Protestant might apply.

Therry wasn't anti-Protestant or anti any religion. As he wrote to Darling, "I dislike no man because of his religion. I respect a moral man no matter what religion he belongs to. My nearest and dearest friends and relatives are Protestant". The number of Protestants who were his dear friends is amazing. They not only contributed financially to the building of St Mary's Chapel, but they lent their names and influence to projects he espoused and petitions sent to the Governor on his behalf. Among them were leading men like Chief Justice Forbes, Major Goulburn, Captain Piper, D'Arcy Wentworth, WC Wentworth, Major Druitt, Edward Wollstonecraft, John Oxley, Alexander Berry, Sir John Jamieson, Provost Marshall JT Campbell, John Mackaness ...

One wonders what moved people like these and many others to give such visible support to Therry. Many of these high profile men were active in their own Church and, presumably, interested in their career paths and in colonial society's social ladder. Supporting a maverick like Therry, who was anathema to the leading bureaucrats, could only work against them. The fact that some of them, like D'Arcy Wentworth and his son WC Wentworth, although very successful materially, were themselves under a moral cloud, may have had a bearing. To be on his side and to be seen to be advocating on his behalf must have meant that they saw something in him which appealed greatly. His religion was hardly the attraction. On the contrary, that would normally have been two strikes against him.

In fact, probably many of those qualities which recent Therry writers dislike and condemn from the comfort of the late 20th century are the very ones for which his contemporaries admired and applauded him. They must have liked the fact that "he was no respecter of persons", that he too was "the friend of publicans and sinners and ate with them" and, as Bishop John Bede Polding (installed as Sydney's first Bishop in 1835) said, "When it was a matter of justice he would niggle with the Bishop over a farthing". (Birchley, p 97)

The Gospel records that the religious authorities were afraid to move in on Jesus because the people were so attached to him that "they hung on his words". Was the pattern repeated in some small way in colonial Australia? The clergy in general, including many of his own Church and the Government House elite, would love to have been rid of Therry, whereas the people, including many not of his own faith as we saw, admired and loved him and pleaded his cause! Among his Catholic and Protestant clergy successors, there doesn't seem to be anyone in whose life this pattern has been similarly repeated!

6

DOWN BUT NOT OUT

Not only was Therry a prolific letter writer, he also contributed frequently to the fledgling Sydney press. In 1825 he penned an article in the *Gazette* which, through no fault of his own whatever, got him into all sorts of hot water. He was proposing the establishment of a Catholic Education Society as a way of dealing with the choice facing Catholics, namely, education at the Orphan School at the expense of their religion or no education at all. In referring to Protestant clergy, he expressed his "unqualified" respect for them. However, a printer's error changed it to "qualified" respect ... Immediately, an unholy war broke out! In the very next edition, the error was corrected and apologies made, but it was too late. The harm had been done. It wouldn't have blown up nearly as much were it not for Archeacon Scott, a new man who had arrived from Britain in May 1825.

Scott was a charismatic crusader driven by a holy ambition to make Anglicanism the official religion of the colony. In this he had the full support of Darling and the colonial authorities. Amazingly, he succeeded in having one seventh of the land in each county set aside for the use of the Anglican Church — in addition to the Glebe lands already granted! He influenced the setting up of a Corporation by the English Parliament for the purpose of endowing Protestant churches and schools. Although it only lasted five years, the Corporation allocated £91,000 for this purpose. During the same period, Catholics were given a meagre £1,000, even though they made up one third of the 36,000 population, according to the 1828 census.

Using the "qualified respect" incident as a pretext, the Archdeacon (with Darling's sanction) petitioned the Home Office to have Therry demoted from his official status and deprived of his salary of £100 a year.

The Home Office responded accordingly and so, from mid 1825, John Joseph Therry was no longer the designated Catholic chaplain. (It's significant that years later Goderich, who had succeeded Bathurst as Colonial Secretary, referred to Therry as being "obnoxious to the clergy of the established Church".)

A little molehill in colonial NSW had become a permanent mountain in London, with Therry as its unwitting victim. This deprivation hurt him more than words can express. He was summarily disqualified, fired, and made redundant, with no visible means of support.

The hurt is best expressed in his own words to the Executive Council:

> I have not been an unproductive servant to His Majesty. I consider myself to have been more profitable, I shall take the liberty to add, than many who are better paid for their services [Anglican clergy received three times his salary]; but as the utility of the Catholic clergyman consists principally in the prevention and not the discovery and punishment of crime [Anglican clergy were often magistrates also], his services are, however important, often either unnoticed or undervalued.

The Catholic convicts and free settlers were again without an officially recognised chaplain (until the arrival of Fr Power) and without a church or chapel they could call their own, whereas the Anglicans were blessed with a dozen officially recognised chaplains (apart from Archdeacon Scott), and provided with eight churches, six chapels and a residence for each chaplain!

For 12 long and painful years, Therry left no stone unturned in his efforts to be reinstated. Others, including high-ranking Protestants, could see the injustice and blatant discrimination involved. Even the *Gazette*, which was not at all friendly to Catholics, and the newly established WC Wentworth's *Australian* made numerous references to it. Petitions were signed, letters were sent, articles were published, but nothing happened. Even tolerant and even-handed Governor Richard Bourke, couldn't get the Home Office to reverse its decision until 1837, when it had become a total embarrassment to the Colonial Administration.

In the meantime, Therry continued his arduous task of ministering to his scattered flock, even though, in the eyes of officialdom, he didn't exist! Ironically, to the Catholics of NSW, his defrocking was a badge of honour, if anything it brought him even closer to them. As a fellow sufferer they loved and revered him more than ever. What the authorities forgot was that in the eyes of some sections of colonial society *they* were seen as the enemy.

Thus the firing of Therry had the opposite effect to what was intended. Freeing him from any connection with imperialism or oppression, it put him unmistakably on the side of the oppressed, especially the convicts and the Aborigines.

Indeed history bears witness to the fact that where the Church is seen to be in any way in cahoots with an oppressive regime, people tend to lose their faith, as has happened in some countries in South America. On the contrary, where the Church is seen to be at loggerheads with a repressive totalitarian regime, the people grow strong in faith as happened, for example, in Poland.

It is likely that Scott had underestimated the now ex-chaplain. The demand that Therry hand over his Baptism and Marriage Registers, as well as stipends for funerals he assisted at, was firmly and successfully resisted, as was the ban on mixed marriages, which had long been revoked in England. Scott was to find out, to his dismay, that far from giving up and fading away, Therry renewed his attack, with uncompromising and courageous language, on aspects of the Administration which he saw as unjust and discriminatory.

The wisdom of the Therry writers would have him lie low in this situation, go with the flow, keep quiet, especially now that he had no official status. Therry, however, was driven by another wisdom, a wisdom that resonated in his Irish genes, a wisdom he found reflected in the Gospels, especially Luke. Far from going with the flow, he noticed that Jesus became the friend of the poor, the powerless, the discriminated against; that was the side He was on, and was seen to be on. In fact, more than anything else, that brought on his head the ire of the religious authorities, and led ultimately to his death. Therry had little doubt but that this was the model he had to follow, however difficult it was going to be.

In this he seems to have established a precedent that has permeated down through the generations. It is recognisable in the peculiarly Australian feeling for the underdog and the peculiarly Australian attitude of giving everyone what is referred to as a "fair go". The underdog wins sympathy and support in just about every sphere of life. Even in sport, where the crowd may be very partisan, there is great sympathy for the perceived weaker or more poorly equipped side.

Similarly once it's discovered that someone or some group is being treated unjustly or discriminated against because of race or colour or religion or whatever, the cry of "fair go" is raised loudly and clearly. It seems to be embedded in the Australian psyche. Therry's influence in this is acknowledged by O'Farrell:

> Therry has been justly credited with more than an incidentally important place in the history of civil liberties. (p 28)

7

FIGHTING FOR EQUALITY

Early in 1826, as Therry stood at the entrance of the overcrowded Sydney Hospital, a soldier blocked his way. The superintendent, Dr Bowman, a rather bigoted Scotsman, made sure the Governor's suspension was strictly enforced. Although pledging his full loyalty to the King and his local representative, Therry couldn't, in conscience, refuse the request of a dying convict for the Last Rites of his Church. He had just arrived back in Sydney from Windsor to find an urgent request for his immediate presence at the sick bed. His official successor, Fr Power, was around, but the request was for Therry, who was the man's friend, probably his only friend, and he wanted only him.

On presenting himself at the small entrance-gate the soldier informed him that he had express orders not to allow him to pass, and, suiting the action to the word, he presented his musket with bayonet fixed, to oppose his entry. Therry said he would see the dying man or die in the attempt, and rushed forward! The soldier shrank from turning his deadly weapon upon the priest and thus were the Last Rites administered, despite the opposition of bigoted officials. (Comerford, Vol 1)

This is only one incident of many which shows how the deprival of status added to the frustrations and vexations of an already difficult ministry to the sick and dying in government institutions.

This difficulty, plus the related one of Scott's Church land Charter, excluding Therry from the largesse being so generously given to Scott's Anglican brethren, was worrying many people. Even the newspapers took up the cudgel on Therry's side. The *Australian* lamented that a more punitive and discriminatory attitude towards Catholics was becoming evident. It deplored intolerance of any religion, not so much because it infringed human rights, but because it tended "to banish from society qualities that were very desirable, namely happiness, cordiality and sanctity"! Then it went on to editorialise from another and almost humorous viewpoint:

> We wish to see all sects protected and all people left to worship their Maker in their own way. Especially [we want] the two leading sects, Catholic and Protestant, kept up with the greatest vigour. They are to the Church what Whig and Tory are to the state. They help to preserve religion in greater purity. The rival pastors are not only guardians of their own followers but they are a watch over each other. On either side dare they sleep at the post, on either side dare they become negligent of their flocks who necessarily become enlightened in proportion to the vigilance and exercised energies of their ministry of grace.

This interesting slant on tolerance and ecumenism gives an unusual positive spin to the rivalry and competition between pastors of different religions.

The campaign for justice and some semblance of religious equality and freedom that Therry waged without let-up for many years was joined by many other people of good will. It had little effect during Darling's time as Governor. But when Sir Richard Bourke took over as Governor in 1831, the winds of change began to blow. "The attempt to select any one Church as the exclusive object of public endowment ... would not long be tolerated." Bourke was opposed to the Anglican monopoly, not for religious reasons but because, like the editorial in the *Australian* newspaper quoted above, he felt it wasn't good for the social health of the colony. His *Church Act* of 1836, providing an equitable division of public funds for the support of the main religious denominations, delighted Catholics. Not only did it secure the much-needed funding, but it gave them recognition and status in the community.

This was very important to them. They felt looked down upon as poor and second-class, and general misfits. Rev John Dunmore Lang, a very prominent Calvinist minister, expressed what seemed to be the general feeling in high places towards Catholics. He had a big vision for Australia but it didn't include Catholics:

A new and great nation which is destined to extend the illustrious name, the noble language, the equitable laws and the Protestant religion of Britain over the Southern Hemisphere.

Paranoid about the possibility of Irish Catholics becoming a force in the new colony, Lang returned repeatedly to the old country to bring out people of Protestant persuasion from Scotland, Northern Ireland and even Germany. In his newspaper the *Colonist*, he expressed — perhaps in more extreme and strident terms — the bigotry and discrimination coming through other developing media outlets, like the *Gazette* and the *Herald*.

It is interesting to note that when celebrating its 175th anniversary in 1997, the Fairfax historian, Gavan Souter, very honestly admitted that in 1830 the *Herald* sided with the Protestant ascendancy against "emancipists, penal reformers, Catholics and blacks". One of its four basic principles was "a belief in Christianity (definitely Protestantism, not Catholicism)". It is only in fairly recent times that it has shed its reputation as "a paper for Protestants". (*SMH*, 2/12/1997)

The *Australian* was a more middle-of-the-road paper regarding religion.

The *Church Act* placing Catholics on a more or less equal footing with their brothers and sisters in other denominations was a big boost indeed.

Equality was a matter of great moment for Therry, not just equal treatment of Protestants and Catholics, but the more basic human equality of all men and women, from the convict awaiting execution to the Governor, from the Parramatta Factory worker's baby born out of wedlock to the medal-bedecked Superintendent of the Hyde Park Barracks. Among favourite extracts from his much loved John's Gospel was the remarkable incident of Jesus washing his disciples' feet. For Therry that was a loud statement of radical equality, equality of all men and women, no matter what their status or colour or rank or lack thereof.

The slave and the master, the convict and the general, the deprived Aborigine and the squatter, the beggar and the priest were each of equal value and worth and dignity before God. Whether they were sophisticated and lettered and at home in civilised society, or were uncouth and illiterate and ill at ease in polite circles (as most of his flock and most Aborigines were), their worth as human beings was not only the same, but had to be *acknowledged* as the same. He was fully aware that most convicts, whether Irish or English, and all indigenous people were victims of imperialism of one form or another, whether political or economic or social. They didn't have access to the amenities and services, especially the educational opportunities, that were readily available to the wealthy and the powerful.

This passion for equality is another of the Therry traits that, fortunately, has been transmitted down through the generations. Called egalitarianism, it is a core value of Australian society. It has to be learned or absorbed by those who come from societies with a class structure. It is one Gospel principle that has become a distinctive part of the culture.

> You call me Lord and Master rightly; so I am. If, then, the Lord, and Master has washed your feet, you should wash each other's feet. (John, 13:14)

Therry inscribed these words in his mind and heart. There they challenged him, especially at those dark times when he was tempted to give up or to take the more comfortable line of least resistance.

8

TO CHURCH OR BE FLOGGED

At Therry's first gathering in Sydney Town in 1820, he was apprised of a practice that was causing much distress to many Protestants and acute suffering to most Catholics. Indeed its effects may have filtered down to our own time. It may well be a reason why contemporary Australian Christianity has a high proportion of nominal adherence and a very low percentage of regular Church involvement. The practice had to do with compulsory Church attendance. All convicts were compelled to attend Church service on Sundays. If Therry were available, Catholics were brought to Mass; otherwise, it was Protestant service for all. Conscientious objection was not considered. As the military saw it, Church attendance encouraged desirable qualities like submission and responsibility, and so it was good for discipline and rehabilitation. In other words, the authorities were moved by behavioural rather than religious motives. Although some may have benefited from the practice, in general, enforced Church attendance was found to be counterproductive.

Therry experienced this many times. For example, when he visited a family called McAlister to the north of Sydney Town:

> There happened to be on the premises an old ticket-of-leave man called Patterson, who had formerly been in the Iron Gang at Windsor and Pennant Hills. Father Therry said he was going to hold service at the settlement in the course of a few days and hoped all would attend. "Well, minister," said Patterson

explorers had gone up the valleys and had been blocked by sheer cliffs. The three got over and came back to report on the great plains stretching out endlessly to the west and north.

Governor Macquarie lost no time in organising the herculean task of building some kind of bullock track. The hard work was the domain of the iron gangs of convicts who worked from sunrise to sunset six days a week. At one point, the work was so arduous and the rations given by the Government so short that scarcely a man in the gang had a bite for three days, till the next ration arrived! The work, however, had to go on, regardless. Any unauthorised stopping or falling behind resulted in severe flogging.

When the track was completed, the Governor himself was among the earliest venturers over the top and into the west, planting the flag on a river bank at a spot he named after Colonial Secretary Bathurst. To the river he gave his own name, as he did to many landmarks in NSW.

The track got a lot of use, but was still dangerous and difficult when Ralph Endtwistle, an Englishman and a Catholic, was returning to Bathurst with a load of supplies for the prison which had been established there soon after the track was made.

When at last they reached the Macquarie River after days of hot, dusty and laborious crisscrossing of the Blue Mountains, they couldn't resist peeling off and splashing and frolicking in the cool waters.

Now it happened that Governor Darling, who was making a tour of the district with a party that included some ladies, came by at the wrong moment. Although the men frolicking in the water were unaware that His Excellency and company were anywhere nearer than Sydney Town, they were arraigned before a magistrate and ordered to be flogged for daring to do such a dastardly thing before the shocked eyes of the imperious Darling and his ladies — none of whom, it transpired, had seen the incident.

When bared for the lash, Endtwistle's skin was seen to be smooth and unmarked. He had never been flogged before, he was making a good fist of his life and was awaiting his ticket of leave. As the soldiers got into their stride, his back and shoulders were lacerated and bleeding and, before long, had been transformed into a mass of raw flesh. Eventually, it would heal, but the telltale unsightly scars and crosshatched welts would remain, making reinstatement into the ranks of respectability just about impossible. Therry was only too familiar with this tragic scenario. Too often he had seen promising men, who were really trying to make something of themselves, arraigned for some minor insubordination and indelibly branded for life.

Losing hope of making a comeback, Endtwistle opted for a path of revenge and crime. Getting together several others of like mind, he embarked on a mad expedition of reprisal. For a whole month they scoured the countryside, seizing arms and causing general mayhem. Eventually, after a couple of people were killed, they were out-manoeuvred and had to surrender. They were tried at Bathurst on October 30th 1830 and sentenced to be hanged three days later on November 2nd.

Therry knew Endtwistle, the only Catholic in the group. When he heard the news, he immediately headed west over the Blue Mountains. The track was particularly bad, so much so that he had only got as far as a milestone marked Blaxland when he lost his only horse.

The next 60 km he did on foot, through what are now beautiful places like Springwood, Hazelbrook, Blackheath, Mount Victoria and Hartley (and what was then the roughest, toughest mountain terrain imaginable). He was lucky to hitch a ride on a dray some 20 km west of Hartley, arriving at nightfall on November 1st, after completing the 200 km journey in a record three days. He went straight to the prison and spent most of the night there. Since it was the Feast of all the Saints in Heaven (All Hallows), it was easy to reflect on life's meaning and purpose, the ultimate things, the things that really matter, God's bottom line for all of us. Next day (All Souls Day) Therry's was a benign comforting presence as he administered the Last Rites to Endtwistle, facing the scaffold.

The man had no family or friends present. They were all on the other side of the world, quite unaware of what was going on. As he did for so many others in similar circumstances, Therry represented that other world of family and friends, caring, loving, forgiving and accepting. He communicated to the condemned man a sense of respect and esteem and a sense of hope and trust in the goodness and mercy of God. As he caught Therry's eyes, Endtwistle could see reflected in them the great beyond, the mansions of Heaven, the place of resurrection and life. This he was able to take with him, as so many others like him had done.

The register in the Anglican Church at Kelso (near Bathurst) has the rather grim entry: "Ralph Endtwistle hanged at Bathurst on November 2nd attended by Rev Mr Therry."

This was Therry's first recorded visit to Bathurst; many others were to follow in the early 1830s when Bathurst consisted of a couple of mud houses, six brick cottages occupied by the military, and the convict prison complex with its own lumberyard. At this time Therry heard the exciting news that Charles Sturt had traced the headwaters of the Murray and the Darling and found they formed one vast interlacing system, draining over half of eastern Australia. This was a great breakthrough. The mystery of the unique river system that had baffled everyone up to then had been solved. It resulted in many pioneers moving their flocks further and further out into the vast uncharted interior.

9

THE GRANDIOSE CHAPEL

On his frequent rides on the newly carved-out (Old) South Head Road, Governor Macquarie couldn't help but notice the piece of scrub on the side of the track. It was unreclaimed bushland, rocky, sloping, and somewhat of an eyesore. It was well out of Sydney Town, which was developing towards the west of the Tank Stream, not towards the east, where this land lay. The close proximity of the new convict Hyde Park barracks and stockade and the heaps of debris from road building made it even more unpleasant. Ironically, this piece of real estate was to become all-important to the Catholics of NSW. When Therry and Conolly requested a site for a Catholic chapel shortly after their arrival in 1820, that was the site suggested.

Therry had requested a much more central location in what is now Church Hill, in the Town proper, but the deputy Surveyor General, James Meehan, himself an Irish Catholic, refused. The reason for the refusal is interesting: if a chapel were built where Therry wanted, "the sight of all the poor of the Town" (Therry's flock coming and going to the chapel) would be much too repugnant for the Governor's eyes as he passed by on his way to Church at St Philip's!

Catholics must bless providence for allowing this kind of sophistry to become the occasion for being allocated what was then a throwaway piece of useless scrub and is today one of the finest and most desirable sites in all Sydney! (Or did Meehan, who knew every inch of Sydney's contours, deliberately direct Therry to this location, knowing its potential?)

Monday October 29th of the following year, 1821, was a gala day in Sydney, one which the old historians paint in vivid colour. It was a great coming together of Crown and Cross, Protestant and Catholic, convicts and free settlers, to participate in the laying of the foundations of Australia's first Catholic Church, St Mary's Chapel, later to become St Mary's Cathedral. All acrimony and disagreements were set aside as the Governor and the priest, robed in their finest, performed the ceremony, Macquarie setting the foundation stone with a silver trowel as Fr Therry prayed the blessing, backed by a specially trained choir.

Therry presented to the Governor a formal address in the dignified courteous language of the day. Macquarie graciously thanked him and, accepting the silver trowel, vowed he "a very old mason, would keep it as long as he lived in remembrance of this day ...". Therry was in full flight, his dreams and hopes beginning to take concrete form; as soon as this symbol of their faith was a reality, it would be easy to gather his flock around him. Many leading Protestants were not only present, but generously came to his aid with substantial contributions. Macquarie made a large personal donation and promised continuing aid to the exciting new venture. It was altogether one of the really successful and happy occasions in Therry's early years in Sydney.

The problem that had been occupying the Catholic chaplain and his building committee for some time was the size of the new chapel. Should it be large or small? Should he listen to the advice of those who looked only to the present? Or should he follow his own bigger vision and cater for the future? Macquarie and his talented wife would advise a building that, in size and design and material, would accommodate and be appropriate for a Sydney Town that would very soon double and treble in population. "Among Therry's papers there are rough drafts of contemplated chapels, one of wood, poor and mean, probably scribbled down at the insistence of some pessimistic adviser. Another shows a long high building, castellated, with Gothic windows beautified by tracery and a tall steeple rising from the centre." (photo section, p 1)

It looks as if the work started before a final definitive drawing was agreed on; it certainly started before a formal deed of grant for the site was procured. This latter oversight caused much tension later on between Government House and Therry, who allegedly was claiming more ground than was actually granted. According to Fr McEncroe (who came in the early 1830s), while Meehan was mapping out the site, one of his mates upbraided him: "Arrah, Jimmy, don't be mean by name and by nature over a bit of land like that. Shift the pegs out a foot or two wider!"

Like many of his successors in the Australian clergy, Therry was not good at the administrative details. He was very poor at keeping books. His accounting for donations received often left a lot to be desired.

In following the bigger picture, Therry ran into a lot of opposition. The money eventually dried up and, although the building went on in fits and starts through the 1820s, the roof wasn't put in place till the early 1830s.

The drying-up of promised government funding from time to time gave new impetus to the voices of the pessimists who claimed the building was far too ambitious for the time. Darling felt Therry's edifice "was disproportionate to the class of communicants"! Archdeacon Scott, while securing all sorts of government largesse for his own Church, warned that the King would not approve of more funds for a building he alleged was far too magnificent and far too expensive. "Even though [Therry adds facetiously] a house built for one of his junior assistants has lately cost the Government nearly as great a sum as has been expended on the incompleted Catholic Chapel."

Catholics too, especially those who opposed the ambitious plan, were complaining that Therry wasn't listening to sound advice and was overconfident about the growth of the colony. Even Greenway, the famous architect, is reported to have said that "anyone would be mad who would suppose that the Catholics of Sydney would require such a large building for the next hundred years at least". (Columbus Fitzpatrick)

However, Therry stuck to his guns and the subsequent population explosion would seem to indicate that he and Macquarie were among those who were right on track regarding the colony's future and the chapel's accommodation requirements. Most modern Therry commentators, however, would not agree, referring to Therry's plan in terms like "grandiose", "absurd extravagance", "unnecessary ostentation", "tinsel and show appropriate for a rich and prosperous city" . . .

Many of Therry's successors have had to deal with somewhat the same problem when planning the parish church. The pastor (like Therry) is normally on the side of generous space and fine artistic decorations; on the other side (generally) is a small band of very vocal people.

The result can be a stalemate continuing for many years, or alternatively, the pessimists may prevail and a neat trim uninspiring building takes shape, or the parish priest, like the pioneer priest, puts his foot down, and a building of which even the former pessimists are proud becomes the centrepiece of the parish plant.

Therry's love of music and singing could have influenced his "grandiose ideas". As Columbus Fitzpatrick recalls:

No one on earth loved music more than Fr Therry did; he could not celebrate Mass in comfort without singing; he therefore went to great trouble to get the Catholic bandsmen to come and play at Mass. Sometimes the Colonel of a regiment would be jealous of his men playing in our Church, when he would like them to play in the Church he went to, and then it was that Fr Therry showed the world his ability at persuasion . . . in four or five years after his arrival we had the finest choir in NSW . . . It was a common thing to have five or six clarinets, two basoons [sic], a serpent, two french horns, two flutes, a violincello, a first and tenor violin, and any amount of well-trained singers, all bursting forth in perfect harmony the beautiful music of our Church. (Turner, p 48)

Therry subscribed to St Augustine's aphorism: "to sing is to pray twice". He felt music and song expressed something that could be lost in recitation. The mystery, the transcendental, the otherness of the divine is best conveyed and signified in the beautiful melodic blending of voices and sounds. Unlike the Anglican and other Churches, Catholic Churches in the old country didn't always have the time or the resources or the desire to develop music and singing as an essential part of the Sunday Liturgy. There were all sorts of beautiful Masses and motets that could be used, but getting people together, training them and providing them with suitable instruments seemed to be beyond the average pastor.

Therry was different. He passionately loved the wonderful Mass music that was available, the Gregorian Chant, the Plain Chant, and the Classical Marian and Eucharistic pieces which abounded in Latin in his tradition. Like everything else he set his mind to, he didn't allow the hundred and one other items on his plate to keep him from delivering on this. That Therry musical tradition was continued in most Catholic parishes in Australia until the early '60s of this century, when the Latin language was disregarded and English became the norm in the liturgy.

As he prayed the psalms of the Breviary, the love of singing also stood him in good stead. He would chant them, as we saw, on the track, with the inspired words floating like a divine mist over the wattle and the eucalypt and the low mallee scrub. Aborigines who happened along loved to listen, as did many of the convicts. It relaxed them. It touched some deep chords within. Somehow it gave them hope.

Because St Mary's Chapel was still incomplete as the 1820s came to a close, a new committee, headed by the Protestant pastoralist John McArthur, was brought together to petition Darling to reinstate Therry and provide funds to complete St Mary's. It was felt the petition would have more weight if its initiative and execution came from prominent Protestant citizens. Some of the enthusiasm for the petition was due to disenchantment with Darling and his somewhat despotic way of administering the colony.

After much debate about the wording, the petitioners decided it would not advance Therry's cause if they renewed his and the *Gazette's* disavowal of the mistake by which the printer had made him express "qualified respect" for the Protestant clergy. It would be wiser to apologise for what did actually appear in print, point out the fact that sufficient punishment had been meted out, and affirm that a reconciliation now should be undertaken. The petition, dated March 1830, was signed by all the leading Catholics in Sydney (most of them former Irish rebels), as well as by an amazingly large number of other prominent people: the principal officers of the Government, 37 magistrates, and 1,400 professional people, merchants and householders!

The request for the reinstatement of Therry as official chaplain was rejected by the Home Office. He was allowed to fill in as chaplain for the time being, but on no account could his salary be restored!

Towards the end of 1830, a welcome favourable breeze swept over NSW Catholics. The unhelpful Darling was replaced by the broadminded and sympathetic Sir Richard Bourke, who acknowledged that the Home Government had welshed on its financial commitment to St Mary's. But first the exact dimensions of the site covered by the deed of grant had to be settled. This involved a rather protracted struggle between Therry, the colonial authorities and Fr Dowling, who arrived and took over as official chaplain in 1831.

Refusing to give up what he believed was unalienable Church property, Therry was being threatened with court action when Dr Ullathorne, a Benedictine, arrived from England. The newcomer, with his official authority as Vicar-General, following the advice of Fr McEncroe, formed a Board of Trustees which included Therry, a body that could and did make the decision to settle the exact dimensions of the site. Soon after substantial government funds were secured, St Mary's was given a roof and was sufficiently complete to be dedicated by Bishop Polding in June 1836.

(As well as being a suitable place for liturgical worship, the spacious chapel enabled the Catholics to act as hosts for large audiences who enjoyed frequent musical recitals there. The first-ever oratorio given in Australia took place in St Mary's in the mid 1830s, with scores of beautiful voices entertaining over 1,000 music lovers from Sydney and its environs.)

As Columbus Fitzpatrick puts it:

> In suitable and pleasing accommodation, Bishop Polding and his staff, public officials and many distinguished individuals joined the most numerous assembly up to that time ever convened in the colony. (Turner, p 49)

10

ASSAULT ON FATHER POWER

After Easter 1830, as Therry was going through the papers of Fr Power, who had died in March that year, he came across a letter Power had recently written to the Colonial Secretary (Power was an Irish priest who arrived in 1825 to succeed Therry as chaplain). The letter was in response to a complaint made by Therry that some Catholics had been deprived of the Last Rites at death because of Therry's unjust exclusion from the hospitals, the gaols and the Factory. In the letter Power, by this time a very sick man, refers to an altercation that seemed to bring to a violent climax the stormy three-year relationship between the two clerics. Having made some very bitter statements about Therry, Power referred to the incident, which occurred at an execution on July 7th 1829, as a physical attack on his person — "an assault".

Whatever it was, Power mistakenly concluded it brought upon Therry, *ipso facto*, the canonical censure of excommunication. On reading the letter, Therry realised, maybe for the first time, the distress his display of temper had caused his sickly colleague.

Having charge of Power's papers, he could have eliminated this one, which he probably saw as slanted and possibly at variance with the truth, the exaggerations of a man whose faculties were being affected by his approaching death. Was he tempted to destroy it? To his great credit he took his pen and, under the word "assault", he wrote another word, a word that is there to this day: *peccavi* ("I have sinned").

The alleged "assault" has been a real stumbling block for just about all the more recent Therry historians. They have seen it as a grave scandal, with no possible mitigating circumstances. It infallibly points to Therry as so paranoid about his own turf that he is close to being out of his mind! This indeed is a plausible enough position. It is an understandable interpretation of a difficult episode. But there is another interpretation. One of Therry's human traits, a weakness and sometimes a strength, was his impetuosity. (Even the fair-minded Governor Bourke referred to it in the 1830s.) It's easy to overlook the fact that priests, like other men, can let things get out of control and, in a difficult situation, react impetuously in a physical way. The situation may, in fact, be so difficult that culpability is drastically diminished.

The response expected from a Christian is *peccavi* — accepting responsibility and culpability, no matter how diminished.

The situation in which Therry found himself in the latter half of 1825 was one of dire forebodings for himself and his flock. Unjustly stripped of his status and his salary, he felt discriminated against and even persecuted. He was well aware of a darkening atmosphere in Government House. There were ideas doing the rounds to the effect that the colony would have been better off if there were neither a Catholic chaplain nor a Catholic place of worship. Some in high places were expressing their belief that if the Government had refrained altogether from supporting the Roman Church, religious differences would have disappeared by now and Catholicism would have merged into Protestantism! Aware of the Penal Laws in Ireland and the attitude to Catholics enshrined in those laws, Therry felt that this same attitude was emerging in Government House, especially under Darling and Scott.

When he heard, then, that Darling had welcomed and favoured the newcomer, Daniel Power, and made him the official chaplain in his (Therry's) place, he was naturally very suspicious. Indeed, it soon became apparent that his suspicions were justified. Power was a sick man at the time of his arrival on Christmas Day, 1826. Unlike Therry's robust health, his was not at all up to the exertions demanded in the NSW mission. He also lacked intestinal fortitude — something that Therry had in a big way. He wasn't a fighter for justice and fair play. He was happy to accept whatever limitations the authorities imposed on himself and his flock.

And so, unwittingly perhaps, he allowed himself to be used by Darling as a whip with which to beat Therry and weaken his influence — not only with Catholics, but with many liberal-minded Protestants, too. For a priest coming into such a delicate and tense situation to let himself be seen as a protégé of an unpopular Governor, who was perceived by some at least to be anti-Irish/Catholic, was somewhat of a disaster. To be looked on as "a Government sycophant" or "a Government priest" (to use his own words), even in the best of times, would be a turn-off for most Catholics.

Some clergy in Eastern Europe under Communism in this century fell into this sort of trap, thus completely nullifying their ministry. Power stepped into this situation through his own naivety and with Darling's help. In his letter to the Colonial Secretary referred to above, he heaped blame on Therry and "on the families of this heartless ungrateful colony, lawless creatures with malignant feelings of opposition to the Government". Just as Darling tried to use Power to bring about Therry's downfall, so some recent Catholic historians have tried to use this bitter letter of Power's, written obviously in extreme circumstances (mostly of his own making), to castigate and even demonise Therry. Researcher James Waldersee uses it to demonstrate, against all the evidence, that Darling and his bureaucrats were really neutral or even slightly favourable towards Catholics!

Power's favourable treatment by the Governor, contrasting as it did with Therry's ostracism, was bound to leave people wondering if this new man were fully on their side! Therry had borne the heat and the burden of the day with them. He was the only chaplain they knew. They could trust him with their lives. His name was written in their hearts. Whether it was a baptism or a funeral or a marriage, he was the one they thought of. His ministrations were seen as adding something unique — a sort of personal power that flowed from the years when he toiled all alone and never failed to answer their urgent calls for help. To have been baptised by Fr Therry, or blessed by Fr Therry, or to have just seen or met Fr Therry was looked on as a very special distinction, a badge of honour, a sign of divine benediction.

The amazing thing is that even though their personal relationship was anything but harmonious, these two totally different men, thrown together by a series of providential accidents, managed to minister effectively and compassionately to the Catholics in NSW for over three years. Admittedly, Therry did by far the greater portion of the work, but Power did a creditable share, even with his health limitations. It's regrettable that they didn't manage to resolve their differences and work together as a team. Regrettable, but not surprising.

Among their successors in the Australian Church, there have been many stormy parish priest/curate relationships, without the special extenuating circumstances of the Therry/Power combination. In that scenario, the new inexperienced and sick Power, being the official chaplain, was the parish priest, while the experienced and energetic Therry was nothing in so far as officialdom was concerned. If both had escaped the many weaknesses of the human condition, if Therry for example had been more even-tempered and less intransigent and determined, he might have been able to accept his inferior condition as God's will for him. But then he wouldn't have been the Moses-like figure that led his suffering, impoverished people from the slavery of the 1820s to the relative freedom of the 1830s. If Power had had a better grasp of English (his first language was Gaelic) and had been blessed with the normal measure of

11

THE CHANGING SCENE

On October 8th 1831, Therry made a decision that could have drastically changed his life and even changed the subsequent history of the Church in Australia. He felt he had had enough. His incessant labours in season and out of season were taking a toll on his up-to-now amazingly robust health. Furthermore, the religious climate in the colony was changing. As well as the even-handed attitude of Governor Bourke, Catholic emancipation (1829) had made it possible for Catholic lay people to attain high office in the colony. For example, Roger Therry (no relation), an Irishman from Mitchelstown in County Cork, sent out as Commissioner of the Court of Requests, was the first Catholic to hold such high office. The priest felt that the fight for the rights and even the survival of his poverty-stricken flock that had so occupied him in the 1820s might not be so urgent in the 1830s. Moreover, just a month before (17/9/1831), another priest, Irish Dominican Christopher Vincent Dowling, had stepped ashore at Sydney Cove.

Therry felt this might be the time to hand on the baton and return to the Old Country. He had already attempted to do this in the early 1820s when, under great stress, he had written in that strain to his religious superior, Bishop Slater at Madagascar, only to be reminded that he would be leaving the flock shepherdless. Now another shepherd had arrived, a man of considerable ability and a good preacher, and so that reason didn't prevail. Therry wrote his letter of resignation to the Governor, asking for his fare. Even though he owned land here and there, its sale wouldn't add up to anything like the price of his ticket home.

Having made that difficult and in some ways painful decision, he went about his work as usual. It wasn't his way to sit around and wait, which was just as well because, in fact, a reply never came. There was nothing for him to do then but to stay and negotiate with newcomer Dowling. Therry had been on his own for over a year and a half. Travelling incessantly far and wide, throughout the length and breadth of the colony, he had become a sort of idol.

But as happened with Power, the newcomer Dowling was given the guernsey, made the official chaplain and therefore, to an extent, Therry's superior.

The relative position of the two priests soon brought difficulties that in the circumstances could hardly be avoided. Therry would not admit the superiority the chaplain was claiming. If Fr Dowling would assist him in his labours or even act independently of him, he would not object. The familiar curate/parish priest scenario emerged once again. As every incoming parish priest knows, the only way to win hearts is to show appreciation of, and give thanks for, the work done over long difficult years by his predecessor. Dowling took a different course and so the stand-off that happened in Fr Power's time recurred once more. Eventually, responding to a letter from Therry, Bishop Slater laid down some ground rules which made co-existence possible and showed sympathy for Therry's predicament. As happened in Fr Power's time, the two clerics moved in different orbits for a while, Dowling making Windsor his headquarters, while Therry remained in Sydney.

Later on Dowling was to clash also with Dr Ullathorne, the new Vicar-General who suspended him (although Polding reversed that decision shortly after becoming Bishop). Like Power did before he died, Dowling wrote a very petulant letter over the head of Governor Bourke to Colonial Secretary Goderich (Bathurst's successor in London), complaining about

Therry. His main gripe had to do with the Sydney chapel and chapel house. His frustration at not being able to have full power and control over the buildings and the people must have at least temporarily, driven him round the bend.

The letter demeans the writer more than it does Therry. It goes over the Power affair again and, in its strident condemnation of Therry, it ignores all standards of justice and charity. It has a shot at Governor Bourke and Commissioner Roger Therry and others whom Dowling perceives as being on Therry's side. It alleges, against all the evidence, that apart from these men the Catholic people had deserted Therry!

Letters like this, as well as those emanating from Government House in Darling's time, gave rise to many of those "strange and erroneous notions with respect to his [Therry's] character and conduct" that cluttered the Home Office files.

Although written in anger within four short months of his arrival in the colony (January 1832), Dowling's report like that of Power's mentioned above, has been used to show Therry as an egocentric pastor who couldn't abide an intruder on what he regarded as *his* personal stamping ground and *his alone*! The fact that, in any such situation, there were bound to be teething problems is completely overlooked. When a pastor is virtually alone for a long time or is just getting over a recent hurtful situation, like the Power episode, he needs time to make a big and sometimes very painful adjustment; he needs an understanding attitude and, above all, signs of fraternal charity. This, unfortunately, Dowling didn't offer Therry.

A pastor/curate flare-up comes to a head at those points where they exercise their ministry most intensely or where they live. The Therry critics have made much of the fact that squabbles took place on the occasion of an execution or at the altar or at the courthouse (substitute Church) or in regard to moneys collected and how they were collected or at the residence, the parish house. Although it might seem scandalous to many, to those familiar with the clerical scene and hence aware of the fragility of the human condition of the clergy, lapses like this, while regrettable, are not that startling.

Therry was still the itinerant priest ready to travel whenever or wherever people needed him. At least once during this time, his steed carried him all the way to Moreton Bay, almost 1,000 km to the north. At a public meeting in Sydney early in 1832, Commissioner Roger Therry, referring to his namesake's 12 years' work in the colony, pointed out that "during that time no-one was ever able to belittle his zeal or his character". Such was his standing in the community that Commissioner Therry felt "no act of Government would be hailed with more delight and gratitude than the reinstatement of this heroic priest in the position of which he had been so cruelly deprived".

Later that year the petition presented to Governor Bourke, seeking funds for St Mary's and the reinstatement of Therry, carried two new names.

They arrived together on August 17th 1832. One was the new Solicitor General, the Irishman and Catholic John H Plunkett, the other Fr John McEncroe, from the diocese of Cashel in Ireland. They were both to play leading roles. Plunkett's appointment, like that of Roger Therry, was indicative of the emancipation or liberation of Catholics from being confined to the lowest ranks of the public service. Although he didn't know him, McEncroe had heard of Therry from John England, in whose diocese in Charleston McEncroe worked as Vicar-General for ten exciting and productive years. Being with this forward-looking, enterprising Bishop had a great influence on McEncroe and consequently on the Australian Church. Father McEncroe was destined to become the one priest Therry felt understood him and where he was coming from. They became lifelong friends. At Therry's funeral in 1864, John McEncroe broke into tears several times while preaching the sermon, as did nearly everyone in the huge congregation.

On February 18th 1833, Therry was called to Parramatta to minister to some convicts who were under sentence of death. He stayed overnight and was about to take the track west towards the Blue Mountains when a horseman brought the good news that yet another chaplain had arrived. Returning to Sydney, he found the newcomer was a sophisticated young English Benedictine priest named Ullathorne, bringing papers indicating full ecclesiastical authority over all New Holland. Governor Bourke formally welcomed him, using the occasion to declare the good news that he intended to be fair and just to all religions, thus eliminating the domination of any one. How this must have contrasted in Therry's mind with his own welcome 13 years earlier.

In this tolerant welcoming atmosphere, young Dr Ullathorne could hardly be blamed for not understanding the difficulties of the previous decade. He came at a time of relative peace and goodwill. The main battles had been fought. The sword was giving way to the ploughshare. The wolf and the lamb were beginning to lie down together. Unlike McEncroe, Ullathorne didn't realise the full extent of Therry's agonising during those long painful years when, practically all alone, he stood up against people great and powerful, mostly unsympathetic and often bigoted. This had left an imprint on his character which Ullathorne couldn't fathom.

To the young gifted Vicar-General, the older priest's attitude often seemed contradictory, even almost comical. Therry was an enigma to him. However, coming from such different ends of the ecclesiastical and cultural spectrum, their relationship, while having its moments, was probably rather better than one would have expected.

In his autobiography Ullathorne described a mildly dramatic episode he had with Therry a day or two after his arrival. Therry was reporting on conditions in the colony and explaining that among Catholics there are two parties. Ullathorne interrupted him: "No, Fr Therry, there are not two parties." He went on to explain that the parties had formed because of lack of ecclesiastical authority. Now that he had arrived, that was at an end because "for the present I am the Church in NSW, so there are no longer two parties".

It's a nice little story told by Ullathorne with a hint of humour. Amazingly, it has been picked up with some glee by just about all the Therry writers and used to show that the bad old days of Therry-induced divisions and factions were at an end now that the newly-ordained 27-year-old priest had arrived with the full Roman seal of authority! Would that things were that simple! If the cause was as alleged, the factions, might have faded away, but, as every Bishop knows, factions and divisions have many and complex causes and, even were the Pope himself to arrive, they wouldn't necessarily disappear overnight!

Ullathorne's arrival brought the number of Catholic priests in NSW to four. Three were relatively new and inexperienced and practically unknown to the majority of people in their care. The one who was known throughout the colony was the only one not officially recognised as chaplain and not supported financially by the Government. Among the civilian population, most of the leading people, especially Protestants, and including Governor Bourke, recognised Therry's predicament — as did Bishop Polding, who made interim financial arrangements for Therry shortly after his arrival in the colony as its first Catholic Bishop in 1835.

With the arrival of Ullathorne (and later Polding), the first phase of Therry's ministry came to an end. He now had to face major change. The one-man-band was being replaced with many players and a new and inexperienced director.

Adapting to this, learning to play the old score in a different way, following the movements of the new baton, is difficult for anyone, but especially for someone like Therry. Pious and zealous though he was, he was also, as Polding remarked (not pejoratively), obstinate and strong-willed like many of his compatriots. O'Farrell puts it well:

"He was instinctively submissive to ecclesiastical authority although part of him clamoured against it." (p 33)

Many, if not most, of his more successful and notable successors have had to deal with this same *clamouring*. Pride, which has roots in every human, including the clergy, causes most of the clamouring, although in certain circumstances there may be conscientious reasons for clamouring and even for non-compliance. The loudest clamouring however, is associated with change. Many clergy, especially Catholic clergy post Vatican II, find adjusting to change one of life's greatest challenges.

12

"BLOOD UPON THE LAND ..." BISHOP POLDING

On Sunday September 13th 1835, the whiff of early spring was in the air as a group of clergy and several seminarians sailed into Sydney Cove en route from England. Among them was John Bede Polding, a Benedictine, who had been ordained Bishop the previous year in Downside Abbey. On the following Sunday, September 20th, he was installed as New Holland's and Sydney's first Bishop. The ceremony took place in St Mary's Chapel which, from then on, became the seat of the Bishop and therefore a cathedral.

Therry wasn't present at the installation. Polding had already appointed him to Campbelltown as its first parish priest. Appointments had become necessary because there were now several priests in NSW, and areas of responsibility had to be designated. Many people in Sydney, however, were distraught at losing the only pastor most of them knew and related to. Probably some felt the English Bishop was not only depriving them, but was being unfair to the pioneer. (Banishing a strong-minded, determined priest to a distant posting was a strategy used many times over the years by Polding's successors in many different dioceses!) Whether Polding had ulterior motives or not, the posting occasioned a very interesting letter to him from a representative group of Sydneysiders, headed by the Solicitor General, John H Plunkett, and "including practically every prominent Catholic layman in Sydney". (Waldersee, p 194) Although respectfully and sensitively declaiming any wish to interfere with whatever arrangements the Bishop might think proper to make, they felt they should record what Therry meant to them and what a loss he would be to the capital:

On his arrival in the Colony he found us a scattered and dispersed flock but by his preaching and great labours he formed us into a body ... we have known and witnessed his virtues, his toils and his industry ... the days of his vigour and his youth have been devoted to our spiritual and temporal happiness. There is no inhabited part of NSW in an area of 30,000 square miles wherein the Rev Mr Therry has not been frequently seen administering the Last Rites, ... comforting the sick, consoling the afflicted.

They then go on to quote Dr Halloran, the Protestant minister already mentioned, a well-known writer who, while admitting the possibility of error but disclaiming imputation of partiality, opined that Therry was "one of the most faultless human characters he had ever met ...". They point out that his falling under Government censure because of his duty to God and to his flock

operated as a powerful impediment to all his exertions ... and deprived him of a great portion of that influence concomitant with every respectable office held under or supported by the Crown ... Though the displeasure of the Government were still to pursue him for an error (printer's error), we had hoped that under your paternal care he would find that protection and repose to which his long and eminent services to the Church so well entitle him ...

The punchline of the letter was a plea that Sydney people not be deprived of the ministry of the pioneer who meant so much to them.

The newspapers even got in on the act, but dropped the subject when it was seen that Therry himself made no protest against his appointment. The people of Campbelltown were his friends, too; in fact, he was the only priest they had known in NSW.

Noting that Therry had made numerous visits southward from Sydney in the 1820s and '30s, Bishop Lanagan of Goulburn (1867–1900) recalled that many of the old people spoke of the bark of a certain tree as "Fr Therry's Candles"! It was his practice, it seems, to use it at night to show the way in the darkness. Although he did most of his travelling by day, there were many times when a sick or dying convict or other urgent matter had him in the saddle when others were in their beds.

Campbelltown at that time was becoming a relatively busy centre. It had a large gaol and a courthouse which had served as a place of Sunday worship after the tree in the square proved inadequate. People were thankful for small mercies and appreciated being able to use the courthouse, but they wanted a place of worship they could call their own. Therry responded as early as December 1824 by laying the foundations of a new church. Like the Sydney Chapel and other Therry churches, St John's on the highest Campbelltown hill wasn't completed quickly. It took ten years before Mass was celebrated in it, and another seven before it was officially opened!

The financial wells always seemed to run dry, especially the Government one; the people's one, even with the best intentions, was always only a trickle. Therry's ideas about church building in Australia were much criticised by Ullathorne. To cater for the climate in the colonies, Therry felt the church should have a plentiful supply of light and air and therefore lots of windows, unlike the subdued lighting and stuffy atmosphere of those in the Old Country. Ullathorne didn't agree. Most church architects in more recent times, however, have very successfully followed that light-and-air formula which makes for a bright colourful sacred space.

Therry's appointment as parish priest of Campbelltown began on the very day John Bede Polding was installed as Bishop in St Mary's Chapel, Sydney. Polding, noticing how much the people in Sydney were missing their much loved pastor, pleased them greatly by his words of praise and admiration for Therry. "We assure you," they wrote rather patronisingly to Polding later, "the well-earned encomiums passed upon the Rev Mr Therry [at the installation] have been a great cause of acquiring for Your Lordship, much popularity".

Among those encomiums, Polding referred to Therry's extraordinary relationship with Aborigines. That relationship dated back to his early days in the colony. A Wesleyan Missionary, Rev W Walker, complained to his confreres in London as early as 1821 that ... "to his disgust he had seen Catholic priest Fr Therry gabble Latin prayers to gaping black children, sprinkle them with holy water and then have the effrontery to claim them as members of Christ's mystical Body, the Church!". (Clark, p 33)

Therry's concern for the ill-treated and oppressed, which led him to spend so much time and effort befriending convicts, led him also to befriend the Aborigines. He noticed that officialdom often treated convicts as if they were somewhat inferior human beings, less valuable than others and undeserving of fair treatment. The presumption was that some people were unequal and could be treated as such without qualms or misgiving. He knew that attitude was common enough in the Old Country too, his fellow countrymen being the victims of it. The conviction that equality of all people, no matter what their rank in society or colour or status or gender, was a strong Gospel value, motivated Therry.

The convicts could see it in his eyes and in his attitude and responded accordingly. The Aborigines noticed it too. Even Dr Ullathorne was amazed at how Therry related to them, tended to their needs, was habitually kind to them, was welcomed at their campsites, especially the one "in a valley by the seashore about half a mile below our residence". Ted Kennedy, pastor and researcher, who understands more than most how Aborigines think and react, feels that at the present time, as in the 1820s, Aborigines respond with instantaneous

intuition to the undivided heart and uncompromised
allegiance towards the poor. He also feels that the fact
that Therry was a persona non grata to the colonial
authorities was an added attraction:

> Certainly it was in that period between 1826 and
> 1837 when his Government salary had been
> cancelled and the Colonial office refused to negotiate
> with him on any issue, that John Joseph Therry lost
> his own heart to the Aborigines and won theirs so
> fully. I would argue that his seething alienation from
> the occupying power was the intrinsic condition of
> his pastoral success with Aborigines in his
> disfranchised position. (Kennedy)

Eris O'Brien, in his book, notes that in 1826 Therry
made an offer to Governor Darling (which he repeated
again in 1834) regarding 50 Aboriginal youths whom he
had baptised at the request or with the consent of their
parents. He would accommodate them in his land at Bark
Huts (now South Strathfield) and attend to their
education without remuneration, provided the
Government helped with provisions and clothing. This
generous offer, like so many others, was ignored by
Government House. Bishop Polding was very impressed at
the way "the native tribes", as he called them, spoke to
him about Therry and their affection for him.

"Nothing is more affecting than to hear them speak
of their attachment to Fr Therry," he wrote in 1840.
Polding was aware that during the 1820s, when he was
alone in NSW, Therry had become very much aware of
their sad dispossessed state, and, when at all possible,
spoke on their behalf. He had tried to comfort them as he
did the convicts and didn't refuse to baptise their babies
when the parents asked. Polding was so convinced of
Therry's influence with them that he felt the mention of
the name "Fr Therry" would open the door of their
hearts.

"If you wish to give them a favourable idea of the
priests, you were only to represent them as brothers of
Fr Therry and the Bishop as father of all." In Therry and

McEncroe, Polding had an invaluable resource for an outreach to "the native tribes". The rapport between these two priests and the Aborigines, the deep and mutual understanding and trust, could have enabled the Bishop to champion their cause, defend their rights and thereby win for them some measure of understanding and justice. Amazingly, at the critical time when he could have sown the seeds of rapprochement and reconciliation, he posted his two key lieutenants as far away as possible: one to Norfolk Island, which had no Aborigines, the other to Van Diemen's Land, where the natives had all but been wiped out.

This was a great disappointment. It is a pastoral practice (or malpractice) that has happened many times since. Just as something good and hopeful is about to take off, the key mover and shaker is changed, or given a new position, or even made a Bishop or superior or something, and so the project goes back into the "no-action" basket, where it remains.

Although Polding himself was much too close to the British Crown to be trusted fully by the Aborigines, Therry's understanding of them and their plight did rub off on Polding to such an extent that he moved a motion some years later at a Bishops' Conference which, in its forthright acknowledgement of the truth, has not been surpassed since.

> We have dispossessed the Aboriginals of the soil ...
> In natural justice, we are held to compensation ...
> The fathers of this Council desire solemnly to lay upon the conscience of all who have property in these colonies the thought that there is blood upon their land and that human souls, to whom they are in so many ways debtors in the name of natural justice, and in the name of the Redeemer, are perishing because no man careth for them.

This acknowledgement was echoed at Redfern Park, Sydney, on December 10th 1992 by Prime Minister Paul Keating:

We took the traditional lands and smashed the traditional way of life. We brought the diseases, the alcohol. We committed the murders, we took the children from their mothers. We practised discrimination and exclusion ...

It was echoed again at the beginning of the third millennium.

We must all remember that not one of these good things which we non-aboriginal Australians enjoy today ... has been attained without the wrenching distress and grieving, starvation and dying of Aboriginal people in the past. (Kennedy, p 139)

This acknowledging of Polding's (and Therry's) "blood upon the land" is an important step towards reconciliation.

13

SOUTHERN SLOPES AND PLAINS

Therry spent three incredibly active years in Campbelltown. The parish included the Illawarra, Argyle and County Murray districts. In Church terms it embraced all of the present diocese of Canberra-Goulburn and a large part of the Wollongong diocese and even touched Wagga Wagga. As well as the care of the convicts and the sick and dying, he had to raise funds for the chapel at Campbelltown, employ and supervise tradesmen, and begin another chapel in Appin. He even concerned himself with other matters such as water. He foresaw that water was a key to any kind of growth and development in this dry continent and so, with others, he urged the building of a reservoir. Finding that disputes over cattle or property or land were causing bad blood between people and doing considerable damage, he felt he had to give time when asked to intervene. His decision, they told him, would be looked on as having "the same binding force as a decree of the Supreme Court"!

His greatest concern at this time, however, was for the people, some free settlers, some ex-convicts, who were moving or had moved out into the vast uncharted slopes and plains away to the west and south of Campbelltown. He knew many of them, had baptised their children in Sydney or Liverpool or Parramatta or wherever. Many of them were leaving what was called the Cumberland Plains with its limitations and were accepting tracts of what was believed to be more promising land in the Airds-Campbelltown-Appin area.

He could now distinguish the various kinds of parrots and budgerigars, and he kept a weather eye out for the occasional emu or lyrebird or brolga crane. The great variety of gum tree and the native flora fascinated him, as did the spiritual attitude to the land the Aborigines shared with him. It was so different from the European vision, which saw land as being inanimate and unresponsive and there to be used by superior, intelligent and self-conscious human beings. The aboriginal view of the land and everything in it, including animals, birds and humans, as one organic whole appealed to him. To think of it, however, as animate and sentient and at least as intelligent and self-conscious as any of its organic parts bowled him over. And yet it intrigued him. It appealed to that mystic side of him.

Mostly travelling by himself, he could go for a day or more without any human contact. But, somehow, he didn't feel alone. In contrast to what he knew in the Old Country, the bush was indeed empty, but it was a different kind of emptiness. As he entered into the silence and the emptiness, a new kind of fullness began to emerge. In the deep quiet, he allowed himself to melt into the noiseless living and growing and self-consciousness of the land and everything in it, à la the Aborigines. The soothing stories they told him about the various animals and birds seemed to create a peaceful, friendly atmosphere around him. Although the flies and mosquitoes were still a problem and he once lost a young horse to snakebite, his initial fear of the bush and the inland had gone, and a peaceful sense of deep mystery enveloped him.

He found St Francis' cosmic praise resonating appropriately with that of the Aborigines:

Thou burning sun with golden beams
Thou silver moon with softer gleam
O praise him, O praise him . . .
Thou mother earth who day by day
Unfoldest blessing on our way
Thou flowers and fruit that in thee grow
Let them his glory also show

John Joseph Therry,
1790-1864
(St Mary's Cathedral archives)

St Mary's Chapel, Sydney, 1834
(Watercolour by Amelia Riesden, National Gallery of Australia)

St Mary's Cathedral, complete with spires, July 2000

St Mary's Cathedral, from plaza, December 1999

(Photos: Courtesy Cathedral office)

Flogged back
(Photo: Jenni Carter;
Art Director: Robert Worth)

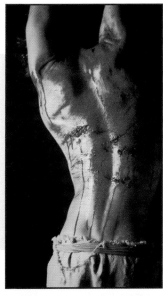

Leg iron

Cat of nine-tails

Treadmill

*(All items on this page
courtesy of Hyde Park
Barracks Museum,
Historic Houses Trust
NSW 19th Century.
Photos: N. Wilkinson)*

Father John McEncroe 1794-1868
(St Mary's Cathedral archives)

John Bede Polding,
Australia's first bishop
(St Mary's Cathedral archives)

Daniel Deniehy, Lands Dept, Sydney
(Photo: N. Wilkinson)

Original Cooma Cottage, Yass, N.S.W.
(Photo: Kim Nelson, Yass)

St Anne's Church "Bark Huts" (South Strathfield) c. 1860
Walls and roofing, original
(Photo: Daniel O'Carrigan)

St Joseph's Church, Hobart, 1841
(Photo: T. White)

Prison Church, Port Arthur
(Photo: Courtesy Tasmanian Postcards)

Smith O'Brien Cottage, Port Arthur

Model of chapel in "The Separate Prison" (for those on the noiseless solitary "treatment")

(Photos: Courtesy Tasmanian Postcards)

The 1798 Memorial, Waverley Cemetery
Burial place of Michael and Mary Dwyer
(Photo: Fr Michael O'Sullivan)

O praise him, O praise him. . .
Thou rushing wind that art so strong
Ye clouds that sail in heaven along
Thou rising morn in praise rejoice
Ye lights of evening find a voice
Thou flowing water pure and clear
Make music for thy Lord to hear
Thou fire so masterful and bright
That givest man both warmth and light . . .
O praise him, O praise him . . .

When at last he arrived at a home, his programme
entailed just doing what comes naturally, talking,
listening, affirming, comforting, advising. His visit
delighted people. It was a highlight, a ray of sunshine.
They felt honoured. They also felt free to open their
hearts, to share the agonies and ecstasies of pioneering, to
explain the sticking points, and the difficult task of child-
rearing in the isolation of the bush. Even more so than at
the church, the pastor/people meeting is at its best in the
warm atmosphere of the home. People are relaxed. They
are ready to get things off their chest, to explain their
anger and frustrations, to seek advice and counsel and
direction.

If they are having problems in their faith, if the God-
relationship has lost its fervour and if prayer, Church and
scripture reading have been discarded, shyness or
embarrassment or fear doesn't have the inhibiting power
it would normally have. They feel that the God who is
temporarily hidden from them has sent them a soul-
friend to assure them of His love.

When appropriate Therry would say Mass. (When he
did so in the home of TA Murray in Yarralumla in 1836,
he was celebrating the first Mass in what was to become
the Australian Capital Territory.) Baptising and instructing
children and adults and preparing them for First
Communion were on his agenda. So also was preparing
people for marriage and even celebrating the Sacrament
with them when necessary. He was welcomed and given
hospitality by Protestant settlers, delighted that he had

included them in his rounds. If they had Catholic servants or convicts on their staff, he would make sure to find time for them. Visiting pioneer settlers all over this vast frontier country several times during his three years in Campbelltown demanded a very high degree of horsemanship and an amazing capacity for roughing it.

At least up to the early 1960s, the main thrust of pastoral care in Australian parishes was systematic visitation of people in their own homes by the clergy. It was very effective in many ways, especially in establishing a good rapport between clergy and people. Its discontinuance has been much lamented. People feel neglected. The ones who are not much involved in the parish feel very much on the outer. Was this commendable pastoral strategy modelled on that of the dust-coated pioneer as he guided his steed over the endless hills and valleys, forests and swamps of his extensive and mostly uncharted parish? Are the clergy of today and their pastoral associates so preoccupied with administration and planning that they're missing out on the inspiration of this pastor who would go to any lengths to be where his people were? In the relaxed atmosphere of the home, no matter how uncomfortable and unfurnished, he would rejoice, like the Good Shepherd, with those who rejoiced, weep with those who wept, be all things to all men and women so that he could gain all for Christ.

In the Oaks area south of Campbelltown, Therry discovered a man named Connor Wholohan, who was suffering a great loneliness for his wife and two children back home. The priest was very happy to inform him of a new Government family reunion scheme, through which one's family overseas could be brought to the colony free of charge. It was an answer to prayer for Connor, who had done his seven years' hard labour for stealing a chicken and a small head of cabbage from a military cart on the road between Cashel and Thurles in County Tipperary — a crime rather grandiously described as highway robbery! Therry told him how to go about applying but, although

Connor had no trouble with words and knew exactly what to say, he had never learned to write. As so often happened Therry did the writing, Connor the dictating. One letter was to his parish priest in Thurles, who had a role in the execution of the scheme. Another letter, to his wife Bridgette, must have moved Therry as he put it to paper:

> ... being separated from you in whom my soul is centred brings forth many a sigh from my bosom ... I have so much dependence on your love towards me to have any doubt of your hesitating to leave your natural country and friends for the benefit of him who loves you as himself ... I fervently hope the time will not be long before you are restored to him whose every act shall be to make you comfortable and happy ... remember me to our poor little children whom I hope to embrace once more with paternal fondness ...

Then he goes on to reassure her:

> the desperate characters that are sent here become different in this country ... there are many who come here for highway robbery and picking pockets who are now rich and respectable graziers, any man can raise himself up in this country ... (Therry Papers, Vol 16)

After many years apart, Bridgette and Connor were reunited, and Connor got his ticket of leave.

Some years later Connor got a conditional pardon, which meant he could travel to any part of the world, except to the United Kingdom of Great Britain and Ireland. In other words he could never return to his native home, being banished therefrom "for the term of his natural life". With four Australian-born children, Bridgette and Connor had six in all. One descendant is Ted Kennedy mentioned above. Strange to say, like the pioneer priest who had such an important role in bringing Connor and Bridgette together over 150 years ago, Ted Kennedy, is known widely and affectionately as "the friend of the Aborigines" and the great defender of those whom he sees as falling between the stools in the Lucky Country. He lives among Aborigines, opens his parish and amenities to them, tries to integrate their culture and artistic gifts into the Sunday liturgy, which attracts a wide range of like-minded people of different religious affiliations or of none.

The Aborigines readily recognise his commitment and love (as their forebears recognised Therry's). They see it in the way he listens to and talks to them and talks of them. They see it reflected in his eyes. They know they stand tall in his estimation. Because he is their friend, they feel included in the bigger society and even in the community of the Church, though they may not be official members.

Just as it is said with not a little exaggeration that the pioneer priest "couldn't get along with anyone in authority whether civil or religious" (Birchley, p 143), likewise the same could be said to some extent of the much loved Connor-Bridgette descendant in inner Sydney! Is it possible to be "the friend of publicans and sinners" and plead their cause in high places and still be welcomed in the halls of kings and prelates?

14

AT CONOLLY'S DEATHBED

John Kennedy Hume and his wife could hardly believe their eyes when they saw the priest dismount at "Collingwood", as their new home in Gunning (48 km west of Goulburn) was called. It was the second exciting arrival in the space of a week, the first being the birth of their fifth child, Anne. Well aware of the hazards of the 250 km ride from Sydney, they opened their home and their hearts to Fr Therry in appreciation and welcome. During the next few days, as well as celebrating Mass, there was catechesis for the other children and the baptism of Anne on August 3rd 1833.

Therry then headed a further 40 km west towards the Yass River, the stamping ground of the other Hume brother, Hamilton. Here the earliest Protestant settlers, the Broughtons, the Rileys, the Mantons and their Catholic assignees, joined the pioneer Catholics, the O'Briens and the Kellys, in celebrating his first ever visit in the far away Yass plains. There, in August 1833 in the home of Cornelius O'Brien (the original Cooma cottage), he is said to have celebrated his first Mass in the Yass plains. (photo section, p 7)

Although he made short visits to Goulburn from Sydney (209 km) in the year 1834 and again in 1835, it's not certain that he went the additional 100 km west to Yass at that time. Amazingly, however, while Pastor of Campbelltown from 1835 to 1838, he made the dusty wearing 250 km trip to the Yass plains on as many as four separate occasions! During these visits, the home of Cornelius O'Brien and his wife Rebecca was a comfortable place to stay. Therry had "a crow to pluck", as they say, with Henry O'Brien, Cornelius' brother, who had a property nearby but who was reputed to be hard on his convict workers.

In 1839 the O'Briens sold Cooma cottage to Hamilton Hume who proceeded to make extensive additions which make up the restored cottage on view today. The back portion, with its beautifully restored furnishing, is the original homestead, where Therry would have stayed.

Although Yass township hadn't yet developed, he apprised the Bishop that a chapel should be built there and a separate parish established to cater for all points south and west even as far as the new settlement in Port Phillip Bay which today we call Melbourne.

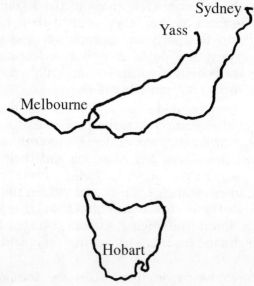

During Therry's visit in 1837, the O'Brien family offered land for a church at O'Connelltown, the name given to the district east of the river. Although it was a short distance away from what was deemed the main street, Therry felt that, being near where the Catholics lived, it was just right. In the meantime in far-away Sydney Town, Polding was negotiating with the

for Hobart. Therry remembered the excitement in Sydney Town back in 1824 at the news of the successful expedition by Hamilton Hume (brother of John Kennedy Hume) south of Yass, all the way to Port Phillip Bay. That overland route was a great breakthrough. It was much used and led to the speedy development of the town of Melbourne, on the shores of the Bay and the banks of the Yarra.

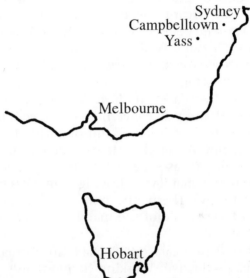

In a letter of introduction to the few Catholics in Melbourne, Polding had no hesitation in referring to Therry as "a clergyman of excellent character . . . in every respect worthy of your esteem".

After a short stay in Melbourne, Therry left the mainland and began many harassing years of labour and disappointments in the island colony.

Because ships carrying Irish convicts did not call into Hobart, the number of Catholic convicts there were not large, compared with that of the mainland. To his dismay, Therry found that Governor Franklin, unlike his counterpart in NSW at the time, was quite unfriendly and was using (even fomenting) the feud between Conolly and his parishioners in order to bring discredit on the

Church. Therry's efforts to settle that feud seem to have been very successful. He found his erstwhile companion in a miserable state. He helped him face death peacefully and in full union with his Church, on August 3rd 1839, aged 53.

Some of the old ghosts of his NSW years came back to haunt Therry during his early months in Tasmania. Polding notified the Governor that he was sending Fr Therry as Vicar-General to Tasmania. However, Governor Franklin refused to acknowledge him or to pay his allowance because Polding had failed to mention that he was to succeed the temporary incumbent, Fr Walkins.

Thus Therry found himself in a sort of no-man's-land once again. He had no jurisdiction in so far as Government House was concerned; so he couldn't make appointments or exercise any kind of authority. Franklin was quite happy to let this state of affairs drag on for several months. At last, the precise bureaucratic formula arrived from the mainland, leaving him no choice but reluctantly to give Therry the nod ... In a way, it had been just a hiccup, one of the many that plagued Therry for most of his life.

Therry's early years (1838–1844) in Tasmania were fruitful and productive. Working harmoniously with his two assistants, the scattered flock was tended, the gaols and the hospitals were visited, and the convicts and homeless were provided for. Societies, sodalities and other fraternities were gradually set up. Knowing from experience that the response to isolation, loneliness and very harsh living conditions is, often enough, excessive dependence on alcohol, he set up branches of the Confraternity of St Joseph to lead men to sobriety and even total abstinence from drink. The fraternal members supported each other in their resolve; they sought together and expected the divine help they needed. This was a great blessing in a small island where so many lives and so many families were being devastated by drink.

Church building was a major preoccupation during those early years. The basic little chapel Conolly had built ten years earlier, which Dr Ullathorne referred to very disparagingly as "a poor wooden hut" had to be replaced and a new church was needed in Launceston. Ironically, the ones who had severely criticised Therry for the size and stature of the first Sydney church were the same Conolly and Ullathorne! The first church he built in Hobart was to be St Mary's, in line with Sydney's first church. However, he found a better site in central Hobart, in a street named after Macquarie, his old sparring partner in the early days in Sydney. Sadly, (as he wrote to Polding), the Government didn't come to the party to the extent needed. This new church, to be called St Joseph's, was his dream church. He had his heart set on it, and, with or without Government help, he was going to go ahead.

Maybe he should have taken the refusal as a sign from Providence to drop the idea. Unlike King David, who gave up the idea of building the Temple even though he had his heart set on it, Therry went ahead, and St Joseph's ultimately became the rock on which many of his hopes and dreams were shattered. Three adjacent sites were bought from the same vendor for the sizeable sum (in those days) of £375. This went on to become a matter of great (and sad) importance for the Catholics in Hobart, and an item of bad news that would make headlines in the colony's growing media outlets. Building commenced in 1840, and St Joseph's was opened early on Christmas Day 1841 — a record surely for a Therry church!

St Joseph's, which stands largely unchanged today (photo section, p 6), afforded Therry the space to celebrate the rich liturgical ceremonies of the Church which he loved so much. On Holy Week, for example, the morning ceremonies were carried out as well as one priest by himself could manage. At night, seated in the Sanctuary with his fellow priests, he would chant the Office of Tenebrae, indicating with a stamp of his foot the moment at which the altar servers should extinguish the symbolic candles on the triangular candelabrum! With the extinguishing of the candles at the end of each of the nine long psalms, the Church became darker and darker (Tenebrae), until only one final candle remained for the solemn chanting of the beautiful plaintive motet, the "Christus factus est . . .". (Phil 2:8–10)

Like its counterpart, St Mary's in Sydney, St Joseph's was spacious enough to become an attractive venue for musical recitals, which Therry loved and which attracted many people in Hobart Town and its district. In an advertisement in the Hobart *Courier* of November 1842, Therry expressed gratitude to Colonel Elliott: "for having permitted the fine band of his regiment to play at the Oratorio last night in St Joseph's Church and for having with his lady honoured it with his presence".

He then goes on in typical Therry style to make a forthright statement which, in the interest of honesty, evidently needed to be made:

> . . . in common with every Catholic in the colony still more grateful to the Colonel for . . . effectually putting an end in his regimental schools to the long-established system of compelling Catholic children, as a consideration for their secular education, to destroy the precepts and abandon the principles of their Church.

Reminding people of the bad situation that had prevailed was a good way of preventing something like it occurring in the future. The situation he was in was still volatile; an explosion of religious discrimination could erupt at any time. The good shepherd had to be vigilant.

Having got that off his chest, he goes on to give an overview of the "separated brethren" that is complimentary and positive, but also very challenging:

> The Protestantism of the present day requires neither force nor fraud for its support — it scornfully rejects the proffered hand of either. It is now simply a

protestation against error, wherever it exists, and not as formerly against the Catholic Church.

What an extraordinary vision for 1842! If only it were accepted, how many disastrous religious confrontations and scandalous divisions could have been avoided over the last 150 years!

15

OLD BATTLES REVISITED IN VAN DIEMEN'S LAND

In the early 1840s, when *The Orator* sailed up the Derwent with a cargo of convicts, Therry, happening to be in town at the time, went on board to see and instruct the Catholics. However, the officer, a Major, deemed he hadn't the requisite government authority and unceremoniously turned him away. Not to be outdone, Therry went to the Colonial Secretary's Office, and, having procured the required authority, returned to the ship. When he reached the top steps of the ladder, he was accosted by the same officer and ordered off once again. Therry objected, saying he had an Order, which he produced. Refusing to look at the Order, the officer repeated his previous stern instructions. Therry refused and walked towards the hold where the prisoners were, whereupon the Major sent for a file of guards to remove him from the vessel, saying he had behaved badly in coming on board in the first place and if he had been on sentry duty he would have shot him!

Inevitably, an altercation followed with Therry alluding to the Major's drinking habits and the Major claiming Therry was cracked! The Captain in his cabin, hearing the racket going on outside "in loud and violent tones", came to investigate. Therry handed the Captain the Order and, much to the Major's chagrin, he escorted the chaplain to the waiting convicts.

Among them were a number of Tipperary prisoners whose offence was "Whiteboy". Whiteboy or "Ribbonmen" was a secret society or Lodge founded to help tenants resist unjust exploitation by wealthy landlords. When informed of the unjust situation, the Ribbonmen put on display a notice warning the landlord or his agents. If that wasn't heeded, they took other measures, like stalking and, if that didn't bring the desired result, they posted an ambush or other serious violence.

They were joined in Hobart Town by another Tipperary Ribbonman called Frank McNamara, from the mainland, who was a sort of wandering minstrel or bard. At this time, the bard Therry was preoccupied with creating and publishing a small book of liturgical songs. Whether McNamara's gift with poetry influenced Therry or vice versa history doesn't record, but they certainly had a lot in common. McNamara's poems and songs, like the Parables of Jesus, were provocative social and political statements on the harshness and often injustice of the convict scene.

His prolific satirical verses revealed the absurdities and incongruities inherent in the convict system. He exposed the religious and racial bigotries with humour and panache and targeted rampant imperialism as the cause of much of the colony's trouble.

Australian poet Les Murray points to McNamara's ballad, *A Convict's Tour of Hell*, as the first great poem written in the English language in Australia. Remarkably like Dante's 13th-century classic, *Divina Comedia*, it was composed at Stroud, NSW, in 1839, and consists of 218 rhyming couplets. In vivid strokes it reverses the roles. The convicts are the ones who are sainted and their gaolers condemned:

Peter, says Jesus, let Frank in
For he is thoroughly purged from sin
and although in convict's habit dressed
here he shall be a welcome guest.

Frank the poet and Therry had lived next door to each other in Sydney when Frank was imprisoned in the crowded Hyde Park Barracks. The year 1835, when Therry moved from Sydney to Campbelltown, had been a bad one for McNamara. On August 8th he had received 75 strokes for destroying a government cart; later that year, 50 more for refusing to work. In fact, in a period of eight years, he received a total of 650 strokes, three-and-a-half years' hard labour in chains and some days in solitary confinement! He also spent some months working the dreaded treadwheel at Carters Barracks (near the present Central Railway Station). The treadwheel or treadmill (photo section, p 3)

> consisted of a long horizontal cylinder with projecting steps. A fixed rail held the convicts' manacled hands. As they walked the endless stairway, the drum revolved, operating a cornmill. For one shilling a bushel, the public could bring in their wheat, rice or corn to be ground. Carters Barracks finally outlived its vindictive purpose and became the Good Samaritan Refuge for women, run by the Sisters of Charity. (Kennedy, p 8)

McNamara brought great life to Hobart and to the prisoners at Port Arthur, when he entertained them on Christmas Day 1842. It was no trouble to him "to throw off a few ex tempore verses", especially when fortified with a few jars:

> Fellow prisoners be exhilarated
> and your former sufferings don't bear in mind
> for when it's from bondage you are extricated
> you will leave those tyrants far behind.

Tasmania had some 3,000 Catholic convicts in 1842, over half the Catholic population of the island. A small proportion of them were political offenders, of whom some were consigned to that darkest and most inhuman "Black Hole" in the prison world — Port Arthur gaol. On various public works they slaved day in, day out, in all sorts of weather. By night their bed was the stone-flagged floors, where they were fastened together by heavy chains. Any appeal against harsh or unjust treatment only led to the lash or something worse. The ultimate was a type of solitary confinement which cut the prisoner off entirely from all human contact. He was prevented from seeing or talking to or even hearing any other human being. He served his sentence in total silence — even the wardens wore slippers and communicated by hand signals. Words like "chilling" or "inhumane" only begin to describe this "The Separate Prison" (as it was called), based on London's Pentonville system. Even the chapel, for which he wore a head mask, was divided into individual small boxes so constructed that the prisoner could lay his eyes on no one except the minister whom he could see only through a narrow slat in front of the box. (photo section, p 7)

Therry ministered to the prisoners in Port Arthur and in other parts of Van Diemen's Land as he had done in the mainland. He spoke up for them, defending their right to basic justice. Unfortunately, he found that the powers-that-be at that time in the island colony, Governor Franklin and his successor Eardley-Wilmot, were more unbending and harsh than those in NSW. Most of his many letters of protest and petition were just "received" or ignored altogether.

A convict wrote to Therry: "On March 5th 1843 I was tried for not attending Protestant service and received a punishment of 14 days and to be kept in hard labour and my ticket suspended." In the 1820s Therry had fought for freedom of conscience in regard to church attendance, and the law, as we saw, had been changed in Governor Brisbane's time. However, he had had to deal with those overseers who disregarded the changed law, until the practice was eventually weeded out on the mainland.

In Tasmania, supervisors and other officials, by and large, still refused to acknowledge freedom of conscience and were causing much trauma to some of his flock. Some officials resisted his overtures and institutions were sometimes closed to him. However, as in the *Orator* incident above, that didn't always prevent him from getting through. There was a back door to most institutions. Frequently, the guard might be susceptible to having his palm greased, and very few could withstand Therry's eloquent and moving appeals. When all else failed and some prisoner was in dire straits, the priest could explode some linguistic fireworks!

In May 1841 the convict ship *Mary Ann* brought, among others, 30 Catholic children, offspring of convict mothers. They were sent to the Queen's Orphan School, a government institution run by Rev Ewing, an Anglican minister. As with similar institutions in NSW in Therry's early days, Catholic children were only accepted on condition that they be brought up in the Anglican faith. Therry, who had already been through all this on the mainland and who had made several protests to the Government about it since coming to the island, took the matter into his own hands. He could see no other way except to gatecrash, which he did, gathering the Catholic children together for religious instruction, or "Catholic Scripture", as we call it today.

Reverend Ewing was ropeable. Several times he had refused Therry access to the Catholic children. He had even refused to allow Therry to administer the Last Rites to a dying Catholic boy of 11 years, at the mother's urgent request.

Catholic parents were often angry with Therry, even chiding him for not being assertive enough on behalf of their children. One of them wrote on October 16th 1840, "There is not a single school in Hobart to which a Catholic child can be sent without apostatising from the Church, whose interests are committed to your keeping...".

At his wit's end, he decided matters had to be brought to a head. As usual quite an altercation followed between himself and Rev Ewing. The latter angrily accused Therry of forced entry, while Therry claimed in quite fiery language that the Headmaster was exercising "spiritual tyranny" in denying him proper access to his flock. Reverend Ewing complained bitterly to the Governor.

Not only did Therry pen copious complaints, but he also lobbied fair-minded Protestants, 163 of whom signed a petition protesting his exclusion from the Orphan

School. The Government did eventually concede that Catholic children could be exempted from Protestant instruction, but this wasn't enforced and, therefore, not observed. Therry even went so far as to offer his Presbytery as a Catholic orphanage on condition that the Government give permission and come to the party financially. "The house in which I reside has been purchased and greatly improved by me ... it is fit at present for the reception of 50 children ... I shall have great pleasure in immediately vacating at my sole risk in favour of the poor children ..." Alas, the generous offer was turned down, and so he felt he had no option left but to build a special school for Catholic children. Thus he prepared a site near St Joseph's Church for the first of three Catholic schools to be opened in Van Diemen's Land.

Eventually, on March 1st 1844, a new Headmaster, a layman, was appointed to the Orphan School, and what Therry had fought for so hard and so long was at last allowed. He was welcome to instruct Catholic children in their own faith. But, it was the old story over again. After he had held the line on his own against all odds, and the hard-won peace was in sight, once again, another stepped in to enjoy the fruits of his labour. He was going to be replaced, this time by a Bishop!

16

THE STRUGGLE WITH THE BISHOP

Much as he thrived on the constant journeying hither and thither in the tepid and uncertain island weather, and much as he savoured the continuing fight for justice for convicts and others, Therry's health was showing some cracks. In 1841, after he had undergone surgery, he wrote to Polding suggesting that Tasmania needed a Bishop of its own, who would recruit priests for the island. In which case he (Therry), now in his mid 50s, could take life a bit easier and even retire, if that were feasible. With that on the agenda, Polding set sail for Rome in 1842, accompanied by Dr Ullathorne. He hoped Ullathorne would become the new Bishop and was very disappointed when he refused. Thus Robert William Willson was ordained Bishop of Hobart on October 27th 1842, in Birmingham. He didn't arrive in Hobart, however, for two more years.

During that time Therry, as we saw, got a new lease of life. He went on a veritable spending spree ... until, as so often happened, the wells ran dry. By the time the new Bishop arrived, they were very dry, indeed! In the meantime, much had gone on overseas that Therry may not have been privy to. Ullathorne was continuing a mild but gentlemanly campaign against Therry. His main complaint was Therry's "want of management in temporal affairs". Therry's presence there was the reason he gave for turning down the offer to become Bishop of Hobart. Perhaps he also had his eye on a more prestigious See (he eventually became Archbishop of Birmingham). Be that as it may, the tragedy was that he passed on to his very good friend, Dr Willson, his own negative feelings about Therry.

We know that negative feelings, when passed on, can so close the mind and heart of the third person that only the negative remains; the positive can disappear altogether. So much does this seem to have happened that Willson demanded from Polding that Therry be removed from the island totally, with all his goods and chattels, before Willson took up duty! Although he promised to do so, Polding didn't comply. Perhaps he felt it wouldn't be quite fair or canonical to summarily remove the one who had in a short few years so raised the standard of the island Church that it was now ready to become an episcopal See. In hindsight, we now know that, had this been done, it would have saved much pain and hassle, not to mention scandal.

When Willson stepped ashore on April 11th 1844, he was very angry at finding Therry still ensconced. He had taken it for granted he would be long gone. Therry, who inexplicably seems to have made no attempt to organise a proper welcome for the new Bishop, faced a very tense encounter, one far worse than any he had faced on the mainland. His new superior had judged and condemned him without even seeing him or hearing anything of his side of the story! It was a very unenviable predicament. The vibes coming from the new Bishop were unmistakable. Instead of the warm gentle breeze that one could expect in such a situation, a cold southerly-buster hit his heart. He felt like a religious pariah, un-needed, unwanted.

His natural inclination to disappear and look for a parish on the mainland could not be followed, mainly because of St Joseph's Church. Money had to be borrowed for Church land and buildings, and those who were guarantors for that money had to be taken care of; so he had to stay to make sure that this was done. This was not going to be easy because Bishop Willson had made another very unusual demand, probably with Therry and his "want of management in temporal affairs" in mind. He wanted the diocese to be debt-free. He would not accept legal responsibility for debts incurred before he took over as Bishop.

Willson was taken on a tour of the unfinished plant: the completed St Joseph's Church (the site of which had not yet been paid for); the beginnings of some other buildings and a presbytery being constructed and, at the other end of town, foundations marked out for another school, church and presbytery. As well as the deeds, the new Bishop demanded to see all the documentation: the accounts, the contracts, what had been paid, what was still owing, etc. Unfortunately, the priest and his friends were unwilling, and perhaps unable, to produce the exact records. They decided to stall until the Bishop indicated his acceptance of the debt.

Although Therry had been forewarned by Polding that his office as Polding's Vicar-General for Tasmania would lapse when Bishop Willson took over, he probably fully expected to be reappointed as Willson's Vicar-General. It stood to reason. He was the obvious one among the few Island clergy; and none of the clergy Willson had brought with him had any experience or knowledge of Tasmania or, indeed, of the Church in the colonies. However, in Church politics as elsewhere, it's not unheard of for reason and logic to be sacrificed on the altar of misinformation and hearsay. Therry was not reappointed.

He was unceremoniously dumped. His place taken by Fr William Hall, a newcomer, totally unacquainted with the penal colony. As well as losing office, Therry now had a much bigger problem — as usual, a financial one! With the office, he lost the £600 a year from the Government that went with it, the money he was relying on to help pay off his debts! It was not a new experience for him, but this time the implications were more troubling.

When explaining his refusal to hand over the deeds, Therry pointed out the fact that two laymen had made loans of considerable sums and, with himself, were guarantors for other moneys borrowed. Therry felt these men especially had to be looked after. The Bishop didn't think so. The trustees "had better look after themselves", because the Bishop was certainly not going to do so. This was a real sticking-point for Therry. Even Polding held there was no precedent that would justify this attitude in an incoming Bishop.

Feeling that he was bound in conscience to protect his friends, Therry put his foot down, and when a fiercely determined Irishman puts his foot down for what he considers compelling reasons, not even St Patrick himself could lift it! Thus began an impasse that was to last an incredible 13 years and defy all attempts at resolution. Everyone who was anyone had a go, beginning with Polding, now an Archbishop.

As early as September 1844, Therry and the other trustees were arraigned before the Archbishop, the Bishop, and Fr McEncroe. The Bishop demanded an immediate surrender of the deeds, while indicating no responsibility, legal or moral, for the payment of the debt. Afterwards, Polding was somehow able to coax Therry "as a favour" to surrender some of the documentation. Although overjoyed, Polding felt he had to chastise Therry for spending so much money without consulting him, for unjustly withholding the deeds to Church property and thus causing so much distress to Polding's suffragan Bishop.

Then came a strange turn of events: when Polding had just about resolved the impasse, he expected the Bishop to bring the matter to its final resolution. Unfortunately, for some unknown reason, Bishop Willson didn't do so.

This sort of thing was to happen many times over the following years. When a solution had just about been reached, the expected and necessary follow-on wasn't carried out by one or both of the parties, and so, with all conciliatory efforts gone for nothing, the situation returned dismally to the status quo.

about the Bishop! This may or may not be so, who knows? When humans, including clerical ones, are at a low ebb, they can think and say all sorts of things.

An exasperated and frustrated Willson did say and write some terrible things about Therry, things that, in the very trying circumstances that prevailed at the time, have to be taken with a grain of salt. Therry had "no delicacy", "no shame", indulged in "religious mockery", "associated with enemies of the faith", "called rowdy public meetings mostly of Protestants", was anti-English, "ran from house to house stirring up opposition to Willson", "attacked the Bishop with maniacal violence", etc etc. (ACHS, 1996) That Willson should think and write thus, in the heat of the fray, is not unduly surprising. The use of this material, however, as an impartial assessment of Therry's role in the dispute, is very questionable.

Willson felt, with justification, that the Therry affair and his inability to bring it to resolution was placing his reputation in jeopardy, especially in Rome.

In the many urgings from Rome to settle, more or less along the lines sought by Therry, he was being reminded — by Polding — that the Therry debt was incurred for facilities that, in the long run, would be of great benefit to the Bishop and his flock. He was getting some hints from Sydney (Gregory, Vicar-General) and even from Rome that he could take the easy option of vacating his See. Even though this was never seriously contemplated, the very hint of it must have been most irritating indeed.

In his justifiable frustration and anger, he resorted to the ultimate sanction; he suspended Therry, thus forbidding him to do sick calls or administer Sacraments of any kind. This hurt the priest very much, but what got to him most of all was not being allowed to celebrate Mass.

Like most clergy, Therry would celebrate the Holy Sacrifice no matter where he was. A Mass kit was always a priority in his saddlebag. Even when he camped overnight on one of his long journeys in the bush, the stump of a dead tree would substitute as an altar, with the wild native birds providing the choir. The desert flora and fauna around his feet and the blue cloudless sky overhead gave him the feeling of a grand church like St Mary's in Sydney or St Joseph's in Hobart.

Fortunately, in 1846, when he sailed to Port Phillip Bay to take over the parish of Melbourne on a temporary basis, Therry's priestly functions were restored. There, free of all the worries of Hobart, he was in full flight once again, caring for and ministering to people. While in Melbourne, he got a letter from a good friend in Goulburn, Bridget O'Sullivan (wife of John), a snippet from which illustrates how much more nuanced was the laity's perception of Therry than the clergy's. She was referring to a priest (with some problems?) who was being sent to Melbourne to assist Therry. "His brother", she goes on to point out, "is uneasy because someone told him you were cross. I said if this were so it must be since I knew you. I mentioned this to Dr Gregory and he said no doubt you would see that those with you did their duty."

Sometime later, we find him in NSW supplying in the parish of Windsor, of which he was the founding father, way back in the early 1820s.

Soon he was back in Hobart again, absolutely convinced in conscience that he must hold out for a just solution à la John Joseph Therry and his friends, while the Bishop was equally convinced in conscience that he had to work towards a solution that was just and fair à la Dr Willson and his advisers.

In 1854 Therry returned to Sydney, where he seems to have been attached to St Patrick's in the city. He said the Sunday Masses there while visiting and celebrating Mass also at St Leonards on the North Shore. Later he was involved in the building and financing of St Anne's, Bark Huts (now South Strathfield), and St Mary's, Concord. In 1856 Archbishop Polding appointed him parish priest of the parochial district of Balmain.

When he saw how things were on arriving in Hobart in 1844, Bishop Davis OSB had suggested that Bishop

Willson had two options open to him. One was to refuse to take possession of the Diocese until the Archbishop and his Vicar-General in Hobart had worked out a satisfactory solution regarding Therry and the Church debt. Had he followed that course, his early years in Tasmania could have been very different. Instead, as we saw, he followed the other course. He accepted the Hobart mitre, took over the Vicar-General's salary, which Therry had secured from the Government, and declined responsibility for the debt. This hardly seemed fair. As they say in Canon Law, *"emolumenta* (advantages) and *onera* (burdens) should go together".

Instead of the initial hostile confrontation on his arrival, had the Bishop (as his biographer Fr Cullen suggested) resorted to a little "judicious flattery" and appealed to Therry's magnificent generosity, a totally different scenario could have resulted. As time went by and things went from bad to worse, had the Bishop followed Polding's suggestion that he call a diocesan synod, things could have been quite different, too. Or had Polding followed Rome's instructions in the early 1850s to call a council of Bishops and priests with power to resolve the matter, resolution could have eventuated a few years before it did.

To say that the Bishop erred is not to say he is any less deserving of being called "one of the greatest men in the history of Tasmania". (O'Brien)

To say that Therry erred in taking so long to accept the Bishop's reasonable terms is not to say he is any less deserving of being referred to as "one of the best loved priests in the history of the Church in Australia".

Was Therry the "souring agent" between Polding and Bishop Willson, as the caption mentioned in the prologue (p iv) so bluntly states (a statement with which O'Farrell would concur)? The answer, in a sense, is "yes and no"! Bishops, like other high-profile and stressed-out leaders, often experience among themselves occasions of strained or soured relationships. Especially is this so when building a Church community from the ground up, in the rather unique and difficult circumstances then obtaining in New Holland and Van Diemen's Land. The Therry saga was one such occasion, probably there were others. When dealing with strong-minded priests like Therry, hitherto-unnoticed episcopal weaknesses, can be exposed. More than anything else it is these that cause a souring in relationships, even in inter-episcopal ones.

17

YOUNG IRELAND IN VAN DIEMEN'S LAND

In the course of their long drawn-out dispute, both the Bishop and the priest were distracted and intrigued by a new situation that came about without warning in the late 1840s. It began with the arrival of the convict transports *Mountstewart Elphinstone* and *Swift*, which sailed up the Derwent in October 1849. On board were some of the leaders of the 1848 Rebellion, carried out in Dublin and a few other centres by a group calling themselves "Young Ireland". Among them were some very unusual convicts, the likes of whom Therry hadn't encountered before. They were high-profile intellectuals and wealthy men. In the gaols they were misfits, totally unaccustomed to the hard labour which was the daily fare of convicts. The rough and tumble of basic communal living and the unsightly mess of pottage that constituted the convict diet were more than they could stomach.

The first one Therry met was William Smith O'Brien, an eminent member of the House of Commons and a devout member of the Church of Ireland (an Anglican). The son of a Knight, he was an ascetic-living, serious-minded husband and father of a young family in Ireland. His people had extensive properties in County Clare (a castle belonging to the O'Brien's family is now a five-star hotel, "Drumoland Castle"). He was a man of letters familiar with the classics, his favourite being *Plutarch*.

Bishop Willson corresponded with O'Brien, offering advice and help, which were greatly appreciated. Through O'Brien Therry got to meet the others, who were more or less on a similar intellectual level. Thomas Francis Meagher, the son of a wealthy businessman who represented Waterford at the Parliament at Westminster, was educated by the Jesuits (who were very much on Therry's mind at that time) at the prestigious Colleges of Clongowes Wood in Ireland and Stoneyhurst in England. One of the most renowned orators of his day, he had his death sentence commuted to transportation for life. His words from the dock bring into some sort of focus the motives which blinded these men of '48, these university men, men from the professions, landowners — blinded them to their own natural self-interest and landed them in convict cells in Van Diemen's Land:

> To lift this Ireland up, — to make her a benefactress to humanity, instead of what she has become, the meanest beggar in the world — to restore to her, her native powers and her ancient constitution — this has been my ambition and this has been my crime, ... I know this crime entails the penalty of death. (Kiernan, p 44)

Kevin Izod O'Doherty, known as "Saint Kevin" to the others, penned some words about a practice that troubled Therry very much, namely, that of indiscriminately throwing together and treating all convicts the same, no matter what their age or criminal record. He referred to his being

> treated as a common criminal, obliged to sleep with every species of scoundrel and to work in a gang from six o'clock in the morning to six o'clock in the evening — being all the while next to starved, as I find it wholly impossible to touch their abominable "skilly", which is the breakfast and supper offered me ... I bear all with what patience there is in my nature, thanks to my good friend Thomas a Kempis. Whether I can continue to do so or not God only knows. (Kiernan, p 44)

The Imitation of Christ by Thomas a Kempis ranked close behind the Bible in 19th- and early 20th-century spirituality. O'Doherty, a personal friend and supporter of

Daniel O'Connell, was a medico and a well-known journalist. He was engaged to beautiful Eva Kelly, who was known affectionately as "Eva of the Nation" because of her famous articles in the *Nation* newspaper, the literary organ of Young Ireland. After marrying Eva, he became a surgeon of some note in Brisbane and a public health reformer. He campaigned against "blackbirding", the practice of snatching labourers from the New Hebrides (Vanuatu) to work in the Queensland canefields. The Irish leader, Charles Stuart Parnell, invited him to return to Ireland and stand for a seat in the House of Commons, which he did, winning it in 1885. Later, coming to Queensland once more, he and Eva lived on in relative poverty into the 20th century.

Therry and Bishop Willson kept in close touch with O'Doherty in Port Arthur, Willson being responsible for setting him up in a pharmacy in Hobart when eventually he got his ticket of leave.

The one that intrigued Therry most was John Mitchell, a solicitor, married with a young family, the son of a Unitarian Minister and the most radical of the '48 men. If they had succeeded in freeing Ireland, he was the one most likely to become Head of State. His treatise on his life as a prisoner, the *Jail Journal*, is a classic in the genre and was a bestseller for generations. His eventual escape from Van Diemen's Land got banner headlines in America, and he, his wife Jenny and their family were given a huge welcome when they arrived in New York. In fact Brooklyn greeted them with a triumphant 31-gun salute.

The New York celebrations for Mitchell and Thomas Francis Meagher (who had escaped before Mitchell) and the wealth of world media attention delighted Therry and Willson and hundreds of people in Van Diemen's Land who had befriended and helped them. It was, however, very embarrassing for Governor Denison and the Home Government. To add gall to the wounds, on returning to Ireland, Mitchell was elected a member of the House of Commons, representing Tipperary, just before he died!

While Smith O'Brien was spending his ticket of leave in a cottage overlooking the penitentiary in Port Arthur (photo section, p 7), he had a visit from O'Doherty and two other '48 men: John Martin, a Presbyterian landowner known among his friends as "John Knox", and Patrick O'Donohue, a writer and journalist whose diary, *A Conspirator's Journal*, was frequently featured in the Launceston *Examiner*, as well as in the *Nation*. The visit to Smith O'Brien, seen by the Governor as being in breach of their ticket-of-leave conditions, resulted in their being recommitted to three months' hard labour in the dreaded Port Arthur gaol. Therry made representations to Denison on their behalf, without much obvious success. In the meantime, the Hobart Supreme Court ruled that Governor Denison acted ultra vires in gaoling them.

Among the pre-publication rumours doing the rounds as O'Donohue was about to publish (early 1850) the convict newspaper the *Irish Exile*, was that the new paper would weigh into the dispute between the Bishop and the priest, on the side of the latter, the convicts' friend. In a letter to O'Doherty written just weeks after arriving in Van Diemen's Land, O'Donohue mentions the dispute in a very sarcastic tone, indicating how baffling it was to newcomers and how divisive it was in the Church community:

> [Rev Fr Therry] had been formerly the sole Clergyman here and erected a very pretty Chapel at a large expense, — he still resides in the town but does not officiate and he claims from the Bishop compensation for building the Chapel ...

He then goes on to explain that the supporters of the Bishop and the supporters of the Priest "seem to hate one another with a keen cordiality!". O'Donohue sought to avoid getting involved in one side or the other because

> both parties have been kind to me ... in my present position it would not do to repulse anyone who speaks to me under the mask of friendship. (Kiernan, p 68)

The question that engaged Therry and Willson's minds and, indeed, the minds of all who got to know these unlikely convicts was why they sacrificed comfortable secure prestigious careers? As Mitchell wrote:

> no man proudly mounts the scaffold, or coolly faces a felon's death, or walks with his head high and defiance on his tongue into a cell on a convict hulk, for nothing. No man, let him be as young and as vain as you will, can do this in the wanton-ness of youth or the intoxication of vanity. (*Jail Journal*, XLVI)

Therry, well aware that the United Irishmen of '98 had been railing against the evils of Imperialism, now with great sadness discovered that the famine was the tragedy that had driven these '48 Young Irelanders to their cells in Van Diemen's Land.

Beginning with the potato crop failure in 1845, it was called the Great Famine, to distinguish it from the other six famines that preceded it in the 1820s and 1830s. Therry had got news of these latter famines from time to time, but about the Great Famine — its magnitude, its duration, its unimaginable horror — he was hearing for the first time. The all-too-familiar television images of the emaciated body and distended stomach which horrify us today came to Therry in the writings and words of the Young Ireland convicts. In cold facts he was hearing that one in every four of his fellow countrymen and women was left to die, and one in four of the survivors were rushing for the famine ships to get away.

John Mitchell describes a visit he made to a home in Skibbereen, in Therry's County Cork, where Mitchell had stayed two years previously. He knocked on the door and greeted his friends with shaking voice, "God bless all here"

> No answer. Ghastly silence and mouldy stench, as from the mouth of burial vaults! They are dead. The strong man and his fair dark-haired woman and the little ones, with their liquid gaelic accents that melted into music two years ago; they shrank and

withered together until their voices dwindled to a rueful gibbering, and they hardly knew one another's faces, but their horrid eyes scowled at each other with cannibal glare. (Keneally, p 126)

The Great Famine was one of those misfortunes that is so inhuman, so far beyond the pale, that human language has no words capable of describing it (much like the Jewish Holocaust of World War II). Happenings like famine are what are called "acts of God". They happen without warning and no one can be blamed for them. The Great Famine was due to the failure of the potato crop. But what about the other endless variety of nourishing foodstuffs the land produced, which even Therry's own drought-infested land in NSW was able to yield? This was the nub of the whole matter. This it was that drove the Young Irelanders. They told Therry and Bishop Willson how Meagher managed to get his hands on papers listing the exports for five of the worst famine months. Holding them up at a meeting in the Rotunda in Dublin, Thomas Francis Meagher had declared,

from these you will perceive that England seizes on our food while death seizes on our people — total export of provisions from port of Cork, Waterford, Limerick and Belfast from 1 Aug 1846 to 1 Jan 1847: Pork 37,123 barrels, bacon 226,608 flitches, butter 388,455 firkins, ham 1,971 hogsheads, beef 2,555 tierces, wheat 48,526 barrels, oats 543,232 barrels, and so on, with barley, oatmeal, flour, live pigs, cows and sheep. (Keneally, p 133)

What enraged "Young Ireland" and led to the '48 Uprising was the fact that the Imperial Government allowed market forces to prevail to such an extent that the food that could have prevented a disaster of such awful magnitude continued to be exported to a prosperous and well-fed part of the Empire. (Prime Minister Tony Blair apologised for this in 1998 on the occasion of the 150th Commemoration of the Great Famine.) The aborted Rising of '48 was a desperate attempt to register the belief that: "The policies of Westminster before and during the

Famine had negated any claim it had to rule Ireland."
(*SMH*, 7/11/1998)

The Young Irelanders' grim sentence of
transportation for life to Van Diemen's Land was modified
and even reversed, not through the mercy or humanity of
officialdom, but through the goodwill and understanding
of generous Tasmanians — some Irish like Therry, some
English like Willson, some native-born.

18

POOR MAN — RICH MAN

Among the passengers on the *Huntley*, which had sailed into Port Jackson on a spring day in 1828, was 26-year-old John O'Sullivan, a free immigrant and friend of the Therry family in Cork. He had got a job in Sydney with the Commercial bank and, when a branch was opened in the bush at the new settlement of Goulburn, he had become the manager. In April 1837, Therry had made a special trip to Goulburn from Campbelltown to marry John O'Sullivan to Bridget Dwyer, the daughter of the famous Irish rebel affectionately known as "The Wicklow Chieftain".

Michael Dwyer, the last of the '98 men to surrender, had been transported to NSW with his companions in the convict ship *Tellecherry*, arriving early in 1806. He had agreed to lay down arms in a cave in the Wicklow hills on condition of being allowed to migrate to America, but the authorities, fearing that would make it too easy to return, had changed plans.

Shortly after his landing in NSW, Governor Bligh had arraigned Dwyer and his companions before the Court on a charge of plotting rebellion — only to have the case dismissed because of lack of evidence. Sorely disappointed, Bligh had taken the law into his own hands and shipped Dwyer off to far-away Norfolk Island. When Bligh was deposed in 1808, Major Johnson had ordered Dwyer's release. The following year, his companions and he had got grants of land in the Cabramatta district in Sydney's south-west.

Eventually in 1813, Dwyer had become the local constable, a post he had held until his death in Liverpool in 1825 aged 53. Dwyer's widow ("Mary of the Mountains") and his two daughters had then gone to live in a house Therry had built near St Mary's Chapel. Mary had helped with the priest's housekeeping until she moved to Goulburn with the O'Sullivans in the late 1830s.

This John O'Sullivan, a trusted friend of Therry, became the priest's financial adviser and manager of his commercial enterprises. One may wonder why he would need such a manager, seeing that his one big financial/commercial problem was that he was just about always broke, or worse still, up to his neck in debt! In this, as in so many other ways, Therry was somewhat of an anomoly.

From his very early days in Sydney Town, Therry could see that he had to have some source of funds to create the infrastructure needed to establish the Church from the ground up. The number of adherents was growing with each ship that docked in Sydney Cove, but they were mostly destitute. Even those who were given a ticket of leave to work for themselves were usually so poor that he couldn't ask them for help. Those who were doing well and becoming relatively rich were not generous supporters, which indeed is true, by and large, of their counterparts today. The Colonial Government, while prepared to support the Anglican Church, wasn't, as stated earlier, nearly as well disposed towards Therry's church, which it felt was somewhat alien and un-British and wouldn't contribute anything worthwhile to the new colony.

For ten years the unfinished unroofed walls of St Mary's Chapel in Sydney cried out to Therry to do something. In Parramatta and Liverpool, finding a room big enough to accommodate the growing number of worshippers was becoming very difficult. He knew that these centres, and other Mass centres coming quickly on line, must have churches of their own. But where would he find the funds? Then too, there was the crying need for schools. He knew full well that the only way to counteract the proselytising of his children at the Orphan Schools was to build and staff schools of his own. All this would remain a pipe dream, much to the detriment of his poverty-stricken flock, just because he didn't have the financial capacity.

There was also the matter of his own material needs. During the 12 years he was deprived of a government salary, the ordinary daily housekeeping bills, modest as they were, had to be attended to. There were the several horses and the feed they needed and, as the tracks improved, some kind of gig was a must. As well as that, the ticket-of-leave convicts invariably looked to him for a hand-up so that they could acquire the wherewithal to work the bit of land they leased.

But above all, he just couldn't turn his back on the constant stream of the destitute, the near destitute, the deserving and the undeserving. As someone wrote of him, "He sat with the Breviary in his right hand and his left hand delving in and out of his pocket for alms to the endless train of beggars who called upon him".

In fact this got so out of hand that, just as the St Vincent de Paul Society did 100 years later, Therry arranged with a local grocer to supply a certain quantity of food to anyone who should present a paper signed by him, the expense being paid by himself! An arrangement that guaranteed his money didn't find its way to the local tavern!

Therry was a deeply spiritual man. He never let the endless demands of ministry and the long tedious hours on the dusty road diminish his daily spiritual agenda. This included, among other practices, the faithful recitation of the Office of Hours, periods of quiet time spent in communing deeply with his God, fingering the beads of his beloved St Mary's Rosary and more. People spiritually focused also tend to be more in tune with what's happening around them. This "in-tuneness" led Therry to an ingenious solution to his worrying financial problems

— not so much an immediate solution as a more long-term reliable one. From when he first set foot on Australian soil, he couldn't but notice that the word on everyone's lips, the buzz word, was "land". Land was available for the asking, lots of land. No-one needed to feel "fenced in", as in the old country. A whole continent was being divided up and parcelled out.

Locking into the general mood, Therry saw this as a once-only opportunity, one not to be missed. In this he displayed an interesting and fascinating facet of his make-up, one that has not been well understood. Today we would refer to it as entrepreneurial. In Therry it was highly developed, a fact acknowledged by those of his contemporaries involved in rural land development in NSW. It should be said that some of his successors among priests and the religious in Australia had a similar gift for discovering and purchasing land before commercial development moved in and inflated the price. This, to a great extent, accounts for the many churches and schools and religious establishments of all kinds standing on some of the most beautiful and prestigious sites in Australian cities and towns. His successors, however, were restrained in their activities by all sorts of ordinances and Church norms. Therry, on the other hand, had no such limitations to worry about. He was more or less on his own and felt free to use his entrepreneurial gifts as he saw fit.

It must be remembered that land at that unique time in Australia's development was mostly scrub or wooded. Unlike at present, it had scarcely any value in itself, its worth being measured only by what it could produce.

It was a very different time for the Church, too, in that its legal status before Catholic emancipation was much in doubt. At least, in so far as the Colonies were concerned, Catholic Church property could not be invested in the name of a body corporate, as happens now. It devolved personally upon the leader, usually the Bishop or Religious superior. In early NSW, of course, the responsible leader was the one and only Catholic

proceeds would enable him to carry on with the urgent building programme.

John O'Sullivan came up with what they both felt was an answer to prayer, a large new allotment well to the south, east of the Southern Road (Hume Highway) in what is now the Holbrook area. Although selling property that would eventually greatly increase in value was anathema to Therry, he could see no other way out than to sell several sites in Sydney Town so as to buy the southern cattle run. Called "Billy Bong" (later "Yarra Yarra"), it could run in excess of 1,000 cattle in a good season. When eventually it was up and running, as it were, it did provide a reasonable return, even though securing a good honest manager didn't prove easy. It is a tribute to Therry's and John O'Sullivan's business acumen that Billy Bong kept operating even during the drought of the 1840s, the worst ever recorded, when most property holders in the area went under. Despite "his want of management in temporal affairs", he seemed to have an extraordinary capacity to include, in his already bursting ministry schedule, the skilful overseeing of ventures like Billy Bong and the many other holdings under the Therry name in NSW.

19

SUCCUMBING TO LAND MANIA

Some of Therry's imaginative successors in the priesthood, in similarly strapped circumstances, created novel ways of raising funds, especially for building and running schools. For many years in NSW, and especially in Sydney, "Housie-Housie", or "Bingo", maintained the Catholic school system. A variety of other more dubious schemes involving gambling were also in vogue. In 1962, lack of funds even led to a Catholic school strike being called in Goulburn NSW, which closed down the Catholic schools. This rather drastic action resulted in the Government of the day coming to the party with financial aid to Catholic and independent schools for the first time ever!

In his "crisis-times" Therry never resorted to gambling, but he did develop a much more imaginative and daring scheme, more imaginative even and potentially more financially rewarding than running cattle. It had to do with a large grant of land in the Pittwater area of Sydney between Narrabeen Lakes and Careel Bay. After much research and consultation, he believed there must be a seam of coal running through the foreshores, joining the one at Newcastle towards the north to that at the Illawarra in the south. And he believed his Pittwater property could well be the very place which hid that precious commodity. So the digging began!

Had it been successful, it would almost certainly have solved his financial woes. Alas, the valuable but elusive mineral couldn't be located, and the venture only sent him deeper into the red. It's another indication, however, that Therry was way ahead of his contemporaries (with the possible exception of Rev John Dunmore Lang) in anticipating the future prospects of the new colony. Managing to purchase some acres between Narrabeen Lakes and the beach, he did recoup a small proportion of his losses by sending boatloads of sea shells to Sydney for sale.

Many of Therry's properties, being untamed scrub, brought no dividend during his own time. This was a disappointment, but having great faith in the accelerating growth of the colony he knew they would prove to be good investments for the future. His estate at Haslems Creek, purchased in the early 1830s, was subdivided and called the township of St Joseph's at Liberty Plains. Sold too soon after his death (against his express wishes), it didn't fetch much because it was still too far away from Sydney. Later on it was redeveloped and became the prosperous suburb of Lidcombe. Two of its streets still bear the name of its original lessee: John and Joseph Streets. Over ten streets in Sydney bear his name, in suburbs like Avalon, South Strathfield, Drummoyne, Campbelltown etc.

Just before Therry left Campbelltown for Van Diemen's Land in 1838, Dr Bergin offered him some land at two shillings per acre in the Southern Highlands at a place called Bong Bong. Therry accepted but, years later, when he was out of the red, he directed that three shillings extra per acre should be paid to Dr Bergin or his trustees because the going price at time of purchase was really five shillings per acre. That property lost value some years after Therry bought it when the Southern Road (the Hume Highway) veered away from it towards Berrima, leaving it somewhat isolated. The vagaries of speculating in real estate!

For properties like Bong Bong and others, especially those nearest Sydney Town, Therry had plans that show extraordinary imagination and vision. He had a dream (and even made some detailed drawings) of the dry rocky scrub being levelled and cleared and transformed into towns and villages, with streets and squares, malls and parks. He especially envisaged space for educational and religious institutions. He even thought of beautiful names like Josephtown, Maryville, Andrewville ...! As well as his many other gifts, he displayed some talent even in the specialised area of urban development and town planning!

Therry's interest in land was sparked off when a ticket-of-leave man brought a curious gift to his door in response to an early appeal for St Mary's Chapel in January 1821. The gift was not in cash or dry goods, but a live animal, a cow-in-calf, to be precise! It was the first of many such gifts, which willy-nilly led him towards a businesslike activity considered inappropriate for a priest. Inappropriate, that is, for most priests but not for one like Therry, who lived in times unprecedented and unique and who himself was gifted with a limitless energy that could paddle ten canoes at the same time.

Did he overdo the land speculating? Did he suffer from the epidemic called "land mania" that broke out from time to time in early NSW?

According to Rev John Dunmore Lang, Protestant clergy were very liable to be "seized" with it; in fact, at one stage, Lang's Seminary staff abandoned their spiritual flock for the four-legged ones, the sheep and cattle in the endless fertile plains!

Much of Therry's trouble arose from operating on the principle that a bird in the bush is equal in value to one in the hand! His practice was "build now, pay later", giving his own promissory note in most instances to get the work done. He was ahead of his time in appreciating the necessity of keeping his credit rating high. As he remarked from Hobart to John O'Sullivan in 1839: "My expenses are considerable and I receive hardly anything from the people (but I should were I to ask). The name of being rich keeps me poor but at the same time preserves my credit." That credit made it possible for him to pursue his building programme, on the mainland as well as in

Tasmania. This programme sometimes depended on selling land for cash contributions.

For example, in 1841 while still in Hobart, he was "offering a half-acre allotment to each of 20 persons who shall respectively subscribe £25 to the building of the Church at St Anne's Bark Huts" (which he named Maryborough, the present-day South Strathfield). That offer doesn't seem to have been taken up. Over ten years later he was still grappling with the building of St Anne's, this time by the straight-out sale of a considerable portion of his land at Concord, which was becoming a little more valuable as the population moved west. The resulting building standing at the head of beautiful St Anne's Square, reminds one of the village square church in Ireland. (photo section, p 5)

If, like his Protestant brethren in Ministry, Therry allowed himself to be carried along by the sheep and cattle and land mania of the time, it was for the good purpose of continuing his work for the Church, not for himself. It provided substantial capital not for his blood brothers and sisters, but for his Church family. His holdings needed time to realise their value, and so he left directions in his will that they were not to be sold at once.

Seven years before his death, Therry agreed with John O'Sullivan that selling his cattle run (Billy Bong or Yarra Yarra) in southern NSW would ease a lot of stress and pacify his many creditors. No-one seems to know how much it fetched but, whatever it was (probably around £12,000), it sufficed to pay off what was owing, especially in Hobart. For the first time since he had set foot in the colony 37 years before, he was out of debt!

Although it may be true that an Irishman is only happy when he's in debt, Irishman Therry (and probably the whole Australian Church at the time) breathed a big sigh of relief.

With the benefit of long experience, the church frowns on commercial wheeling and dealing by the clergy, no matter how entrepreneurially gifted some may be and how great the material benefit thus derived.

Polding fully agreed with this church stand and, as was his episcopal duty, pointed it out strongly to Therry in 1856 before appointing him as pastor in Sydney. The temptation to get so absorbed that the main game (dedication to the pastoral ministry) is in danger of being neglected is too great, even for a man like Therry, now approaching his three score and ten years.

When disposing of his real estate, Therry's "lack of management in temporal affairs" showed up once more. He failed to see the necessity of getting proper legal help to draw up his Will (or to be precise, his "Wills", for he made several). The fact that he drew them up himself resulted in somewhat of a nightmare for his executors. His failure to include Archbishop Polding as a beneficiary was a disappointment. Polding had been Therry's supporter and friend over the years. As leader of the Sydney Church, it was taken for granted that he would be the main beneficiary.

Therry did, of course, give generously to Polding's Cathedral Church ... One donation from the sale of Billy Bong had the distinctive mark of Therry the businessman. It was a gift of £2,000, but with some strings attached — strings that indicated his continuing love affair with St Mary's. He offered the money on condition that the people of the colony contribute four times that amount within six months! It was a good try but, unfortunately, it didn't succeed in bringing in the £8,000. When that became clear, the £2,000 were handed over none the less.

The main beneficiaries of Therry's Will, in fact, were the Jesuits. Since his early days in the colony, Therry saw education as the key to lifting people out of the poverty cycle that enveloped most of his flock. His own attempts at providing schools were unsuccessful, because he didn't have the wherewithal to attract good teachers and maintain them. He liked the Jesuits because he felt that, having a good philosophy of education, they were the best in the field. He liked them too because, like himself, they were under a cloud and unjustly suppressed in many European Countries. (Perhaps also he felt that giving priority to boys' higher education mightn't be too inappropriate in early colonial circumstances.) Before coming to the Antipodes, he had met and evidently was impressed by some Irish Jesuits who were still under a politically motivated ban at that time. As early as 1836, he expressed a wish to have the Jesuits introduced into NSW.

In the same year his vision for the Church took a new leap forward to include native-born clergy training. He set aside part of his Pittwater property as a site for two major educational enterprises, an ecclesiastical seminary and a lay college, both to be in the charge of the Jesuits. (Perhaps he saw them as a counterbalance to the seminary then being planned by Polding to fulfil his Benedictine dream for Australia.) Not leaving anything to chance, he directed that Sts Peter and Paul and St Joseph be their respective patrons!

In 1843 his vision was expanding and embracing the peoples of the various islands of the South Pacific who were as yet untouched by the Gospel. With impressive foresight, he directed that the proposed Pittwater seminary should include these people in its missionary outreach. It was to train young men to minister in Australia and in the Islands of the South Pacific.

So it was that in 1857 he directed "(... without the slightest want of respect for the ecclesiastical authorities of this colony) that Irish Jesuits ... should have the management of the whole of my property for the purpose of appropriating its proceeds ... for religious, charitable and educational purposes".

At the time of his death, his personal estate was entirely inadequate to fund the many charities mentioned in his Will. Even though of considerable acreage, the land itself at that stage was of no great value. It could have afforded him much comfort in his twilight years, but he didn't avail himself of that. Making do with the bare necessities of life, he died as he lived in relative poverty. He opted for that poverty of spirit which leads to the Kingdom of Heaven. (cf Mt 5:3)

It wasn't until 1878, when Joseph Dalton SJ came from Melbourne to buy some land in Tambourine Bay, on Sydney's North Shore, that his dream of a Jesuit college began to take shape. On this beautiful site, St Ignatius (Riverview) College was built, followed later by St Aloysius' College in what was then called Old St Kilda House. These two schools have provided quality education to thousands of Catholic boys. The Jesuit Fathers who run them are very conscious that in order to be faithful to their original benefactor, free places should be offered each year to boys from the most deprived homes.

20

EGALITARIANISM UNDER ATTACK

Polding's exclusion from Therry's Will could have had something to do with a friend of Therry's called Daniel Deniehy, whose parents, both Irish convicts, were almost certainly married by Therry and who himself was baptised by him. Deniehy was to become the literary, legal and political prodigy of the colony, the most gifted of the century's "Currency Lads and Lasses" (as those born in the colony were called). He is accredited with playing a major part in preserving Australia from an aristocratic Upper House (House of Lords). One of the first Catholics elected to Parliament in 1856 and a noted devotee of art and literature, Deniehy was described by WD Dalley (a senior Cabinet Minister) as "the most gifted Irish Australian of our history" and by Henry Parkes as "one of the truest democrats that ever lived". He advocated the separation of Church and State (as in the USA) so that the Church, free from the shackle of the State, could exercise the widest possible influence for good.

This was a very contentious issue because it meant the cessation of all government financial help for Church building programmes and no more government clergy salaries. It had been mooted in government circles for some time and was to apply to all of the four main Churches in the colony. It would affect the Anglicans most of all but they were fortunate enough to have a much stronger financial base than the others. It was opposed strongly by Polding and by just about all the other Bishops and clergy and many of the leading laity.

The fact that Deniehy and his supporters and the *Freemans Journal* were enthusiastically promoting it irritated Polding no end. Among other things, he felt that once it started, it would flow on to schools; the abolition of State aid to schools would be the next step which, in fact, it was.

Going on the principle that he who pays the piper calls the tune, Deniehy thought that if the Bishop and clergy were dependent (financially) solely on the laity, they would be more responsive to the wishes and suggestions of their people. This seemed logical enough at the time, but subsequent history of the Australian Church shows that the cessation of Government money made little, if any, difference to the role of the laity in the Church community.

Deniehy was aware of the theories being expressed overseas by prominent liberal Catholics like Cardinal John Henry Newman, who felt the gifts of lay people were as necessary for the development of Church communities as were those of the clergy. These gifts, given precisely for that purpose were, by and large, left unused, much to the detriment of the Church. It was up to the Bishop and the clergy to support and empower the laity in the discernment and use of these gifts ... Although Polding might have subscribed to this in theory, the whole laity thing didn't sit well with him nor with his Benedictine Vicar-General Gregory. He referred to it pejoratively and mistakenly as "Presbyterien", a kind of Presbyterianism aimed at subverting the authority of the hierarchy. It was also greatly at variance with Religious life.

In a Benedictine monastery, the monks were subject to the Abbot, to whom they gave unquestioning obedience. Similarly, in the Church, the laity were expected to give unqualified assent to what the Bishop decided, even if they believed it was unwise or downright wrong. Unfortunately, some decisions being taken at that time by Gregory on behalf of Polding seemed quite unsound, such as refusing qualified laity seats on the Board of St John's College. Gregory was "an insolent man, though Dr Polding could never see it, causing dissension among his own brethren, sowing discontent among the seculars and finally leading to Gregory's own banishment from the Australian Mission". (Hartigan, p 99)

French overtones of liberty, equality and fraternity were being raised abroad in the colony, and people were wondering how the Church could subscribe to equality for all its members in Christ while denying 99.9% of them any say whatsoever in its decisions and in its ministries.

The burning question of the day in so far as Sydney was concerned had to do with Polding's successor. The thought of another Benedictine and the continuing Benedictinisation of the Church in Sydney was anathema to most people. The laity and most of the clergy would agree with the *Freemans Journal* that Benedictinism, as represented by Gregory and Polding, just didn't suit a penal colony and wouldn't work. Thus their cry was for non-Benedictine Bishops for Australia and, in practical terms, that meant Irish Bishops. "English" being more or less co-terminous with Benedictine, the push for an Irish Hierarchy was an urgent practical matter.

To describe it, as some have done, as Irish Empire-building or spiritual colonisation would have made no sense at all to people like Therry or McEncroe or Deniehy. The *Freemans Journal*, the paper at the centre of the agitation, owned and edited by an Englishman, Mr JK Heydon, wasn't promoting the sort of meaningless hyperbole that may have appeared in some pious magazine in Ireland, or may have been expressed there by some over-enthusiastic prelate. The Therry and McEncroe papers would be very disappointing reading for those who would like to raise questions of "Pommy bashing" as we call it now, or any kind of anti-English prejudice.

Unfortunately, Polding himself was not totally without a streak of prejudice. Although he knew quite well that McEncroe was no longer owner or editor of the *Freemans Journal* and had no part in its excesses, he still couldn't quite rid himself of the stereotype. In a report to Rome on McEncroe and JK Heydon (McEncroe's successor as owner/editor of the paper), in 1858, he wrote in French: "Archdeacon McEncroe is moreover an Irishman, and the ready prejudices and bitterness are always flung by the newspaper into every occasion of difference, cause or no cause". (Sydney Diocesan Archives) His estimation of Heydon in the same report has some telltale traces of colonial snobbery: "Mr Heydon, a man of some talent but illiterate, of low origins and social position ..." These attitudes, although not normally expressed, would have communicated themselves non-verbally, thereby leading to a heightening of tension.

> In July 1858 Polding felt constrained to hold out some form of olive branch to the leading laymen in the opposition. He chose JJ Therry to communicate to those concerned his [Polding's] desire to have made known to him the wishes of the people in regard to the administration of Catholic affairs within the Archdiocese. (Birchley, p 181)

The choice of Therry for this task was indeed a clever one; no-one would know people's desires and aspirations and dreams better than Therry and McEncroe. Polding's problem, however, was one of not listening, of not paying attention to what people like Deniehy had to offer. To him Deniehy, a man of convict origin, was of very lowly background indeed. It was unthinkable that he would have something inspirational or something of the Holy Spirit to communicate! Polding would have thought it more likely that with those rebel Irish genes, in his advocacy of a role for the laity he was merely trying to undermine authority, the God-given authority of the English Archbishop. The attitude, "Can anything good come out of Nazareth?" blinded this otherwise holy and gracious prelate to the fact that "the Spirit breathes where He wills" and that "God can raise up sons and daughters of Abraham from these stones". Had he even chosen to talk with Therry or McEncroe instead of with his Vicar-General, he and the Church could have been saved much trauma and he could have set some precedent for his fellow Bishops to follow.

Sadly, the place of the laity in the Australian Church became stuck at the "pay, pray and obey" level. The Irish and Australian-born Bishops who succeeded Polding have given eloquent lip-service to the role of the laity, but oftentimes they, too, have been haunted by the fear of what might happen if the laity had some real power or say in the decision-making process in the diocese or in the selection of future Bishops. This attitude has also infected the parish clergy in that, years after the great opening up to the laity by Vatican Council II, effective parish and diocesan councils are far from the norm. Even as the new millennium opens, the Vatican bureaucracy is tending to wind back the clock by revisiting some of the pre-Vatican II authoritarianism and clericalism on the contemporary Australian Church.

The role of the laity in the Church will cease to be threatening only when the pivotal role of the Holy Spirit is acknowledged and trusted. This "letting-go, letting-God" is extremely difficult and probably will only become a reality when the shortage of priests reaches crisis proportions.

Things came to a climax in 1859 when, at a public gathering of 900 people, Deniehy criticised "the authoritarian and high-handed rule of Polding and Gregory". He moved that "it was neither safe nor creditable for Catholics to continue their confidence in Polding and Gregory"! Polding's response to this provocative position was equally provocative; there weren't any more suggestions of dialogue or negotiation. Seven of the leaders were threatened with the Church's ultimate penalty — excommunication!

Six of them recanted but, while Deniehy recanted verbally, he refused to do so in writing, and so the dreaded sentence was promptly ratified in his case.

Strange to say, on the very week of his excommunication, Deniehy delivered a lecture in St Mary's Cathedral Hall. It was also after he had been excommunicated that his fight to have St John's College accredited by the Sydney University Senate was successful.

However, things didn't go well for him after excommunication. Polding evidently made little if any effort to reinstate him before his untimely death in Bathurst from alcoholism in 1865, the year after Therry died in Balmain. Polding's obduracy in refusing him Christian burial was widely condemned. The *Bulletin* referred to it as a sort of "clerical brutality". Henry Lawson lamented:

> Southern men of letters, seeking kinder fields across the waves
>
> Tell a shameful tale entitled: "Deniehy's Forgotten Grave".

Twenty years later, with Cardinal Moran's approval, Deniehy was re-interred in the Catholic portion of Waverley Cemetery. A fine statue of him stands at the side of the old Lands Department building in Bridge Street, Sydney. (photo section, p 4) He stands there among a pantheon of eminent Australians: explorers, pioneers and politicians.

It should be noted that Therry's great friend, Archdeacon McEncroe, was in some strife at this time. As well as being best friends, McEncroe and Therry were the two leading priests in the colony. Conjointly they set up bursaries for the education of students to the priesthood and many other enterprises. They were different in that the even-tempered diplomatic McEncroe didn't ruffle nearly as many authority feathers as his older friend did.

The idea of launching a Catholic paper originated in 1837 in Campbelltown, when Therry suggested to Polding that a paper was a necessity if only to counteract the scurrilous things being featured in some of the secular press. Polding was interested in purchasing an already established paper, but nothing much happened till 1850, when McEncroe bit the bullet and became the founder and editor of the *Freemans Journal*. This role wasn't new to him. Previously, in Charleston USA he was for many years the distinguished editor and manager of Bishop England's *Miscellany*, a paper read nationally, in which local and overseas news and articles left room for the laity to have their say freely and without recrimination.

"The function and stance of the *Miscellany* which laid it open to episcopal criticism were to be paralleled closely by McEncroe in his own future paper in New South Wales." (Birchley, p 20) McEncroe was very successful in this role until eventually, with Polding's approval, he handed it over to JK Heydon. Under Heydon, who himself was a Polding convert, the paper became involved in the heated discussion about the role of the laity. Some letters were published which were quite offensive to Polding and Gregory. McEncroe wrote in support of his Archbishop, pointing out the errors and condemning the offences.

The paper eagerly took up the cause of Sr de Lacy who, for years, had been the leading light in the very successful founding and development of the first St Vincent's Hospital in Sydney. In the midst of the tension between the Archbishop and the Sisters of Charity regarding the administration of the hospital, Sr de Lacy decided to uproot herself and return to Ireland. The *Freemans* publicity made this into a cause célèbre, laying the blame for the departure of this well-respected and gifted woman squarely at the feet of the Archbishop. This, according to O'Sullivan, who has researched the matter in great detail, would seem to be true only "on the general principle that the person at the top has final responsibility". (p 240)

Because the paper continued to be a strident voice of protest, Polding asked McEncroe to rein it in. McEncroe refused. He didn't own it anymore and, like Therry, he saw the value of freedom of the press, and indeed the sometimes painful freedom of the Catholic press. Even a Catholic paper, he believed, should be independent and free to express both sides. He felt one of the roles of the Catholic Press was to be a forum where people who care for the Church and want to promote its mission are able to express with charity their frustrations and problems, as well as their hopes and dreams.

21

ARCHPRIEST

At a conference for clergy held in Campbelltown in the year 1858, Archbishop Polding made an announcement that would have gladdened the hearts of everyone present. Speaking about the old pioneer priest, he said he was seeking some way of honouring Therry, and gave two reasons: to acknowledge the pivotal role he had played in the Australian Church and to signify his fraternal standing with his brothers in the ministry. Most of his disputes and misunderstandings had to do with members of the clergy, of all ranks. (His dispute with Bishop Willson had only been finally resolved the year before.) Knowing that Therry the priest had been in many ways outstanding, Polding felt a title in acknowledgement would be most appropriate.

Suggested titles like "Canon" or "Archdeacon" or even "Monsignor" would entail acquiring and wearing distinctive purple garments which wouldn't sit comfortably with someone who identified with and was the friend to the marginalised ("the publicans and the sinners") of his day.

Then, one of the more imaginative brethren came up with a title that had scarcely been heard of before, that of "Archpriest", and no sooner was it mentioned than it was seen to fit perfectly. It was acclaimed there and then by the clergy and, when it hit the media, it caused ripples of joy and enthusiasm throughout the colony. Even John Henry Newman, on the other side of the world, was delighted, feeling it was a clear indication that the old warrior was fully vindicated in the eyes of his colleagues and the Church hierarchy.

The clergy assembled at Campbelltown knew that even though Therry was pre-eminently, in season and out of season, a man of action, he didn't neglect that other calling of a priest, namely preaching the Gospel. Preaching God's Word is a task which some Catholic clergy take rather lightly, allocating to it only minimum last-minute preparation. Protestant clergy generally give it high priority in their weekly programme and devote quite a lot of time to its preparation. In spite of his extremely busy schedule and the hours on end he spent on the track each day, Therry, too, devoted much time and energy each week to marshalling and expressing his thoughts in a way that would be understandable to his mostly illiterate congregations.

He could have taken the easy way out and settled for pious platitudes that would have maybe pleased but would not have instructed his hearers, as many of his successors have been tempted to do. For Therry, education in religion had a very high priority. Realising that although his people's tribal attachment to the faith was very strong, their knowledge was seriously deficient, he determined from the outset to try to change this. He looked on the sermon as a very important step in the educative process. He made the effort to become familiar with the great French preachers like Bourdeloue and Massillon, whom he often quoted. He had a familiarity with sacred scripture, perhaps more than the general run of Catholic clergy, and brought a multitude of applicable quotes into his sermons. He was gifted with a quiet and easy manner, and a voice that even in his later years, was both penetrating and pleasing. Sometimes he wrote his sermon in full but, more frequently, he preached from a brief sketch. In the sermon notes among his papers there is a directness and simplicity which show a complete knowledge of the subject and a determination to express it in a way that would interest and hold the attention of his hearers. Unlike most of the clergy in the Latin Mass era, he took time even at weekday Masses to explain the Word.

He wasn't an accomplished scholar, but even in the far-away Antipodes and in the midst of the constant coming and going of his busy life, he managed to keep up to date with the thought patterns of his time. Among his books of dogmatic and moral theology, his library included well-thumbed copies of some of the classics of yesteryear, like *Pliny's Letters, Xenophon's Works, Morell's Philosophy, Hebrew and Greek Lexicons* and Lingard's *History of England*, exquisitely bound in many volumes. Pope's famous *Essay on Man* was a particular favourite. Commentaries on the psalms and the New Testament were frequently consulted, as well as the Lives of the Saints, especially the masters of mysticism and meditation like John of the Cross and Teresa of Avila. He was, of course, very much a doer, like Martha. The more robust activity-oriented side of priesting seemed to fill his day to the brim. However, there is much evidence to suggest that he didn't neglect the quiet listening role of Mary.

He savoured, for example, the most mystical books of the Hebrew Scriptures, books like the *Song of Songs* and the other Wisdom books which see the face of God mirrored in the beauty and goodness of creation. He even went to the trouble of copying these, word for word, from the *Vulgate*. They evidently nourished his spirit and the laborious task of putting them on paper with his own hand enabled him to recall and savour them as he sallied out into the multi-faceted Australian bush. His favourite New Testament book was that of his mystically oriented namesake, the *Gospel of John*. From a French translation he penned every word and verse of *John's* 21 chapters and in so doing ensured that much of it would stay with him, nurturing his spirit and enriching his ministry. To skip over this aspect of his life, this mystical bent, would be a mistake; it's probable that it played a key role, giving depth and meaning to the incessant activity that would otherwise have frazzled him and sapped his inner vitality.

The mystical in him surfaces, too, in his great love for singing, music and poetry. In fact, apart from a very small number of his successors who were gifted poets, he could be classed among the rest as a sort of mini-poet laureate. Believing, as many do today, that song and music can be a good way of communicating the Good News, he did, in quite a different format, what the contemporary Gospel singers are doing. Distilling into his simple rhyming verses some aspect of the Gospel message, he celebrated the liturgy while evangelising in a relaxed easy way. Typically, he responded to the shortage of suitable hymns by writing his own. He published them not because of their literary quality, but to fill a void.

His very special relationship with children is perhaps another indication of his mystical side. One of the things about Therry which James Bonwick remembered many years later had to do with the priest's easy rapport with children. He obviously loved "the little ones" and would never pass by without giving them his attention and having a chat. This love was evidently mutual. At the turn of the century, many of the older people who were children in Therry's time remembered his special bonding with them, the time he would spend, his affection and obvious delight in their company. They all knew him and called him their friend.

When disheartened with the iniquities of the convict system, he found solace and recreation in the children's innocent trusting love. The book of poems he published in Hobart Town in 1846 he dedicated "to the children, by their devoted friend John Joseph Therry". He used these poems and songs as teaching tools, just as today our Junior Primary teachers use Carey Landry and other musical bards to teach the Good News of Jesus Christ to the little ones in their care.

The bonding between priests and children has flourished in the Australian Church since Therry's time. The youthful vitality and the affection and friendship of children have sustained and bolstered many a weary, stressed-out pastor down through the years. Although the easy familiarity of yesteryear may have suffered a setback because of recent clerical scandals, it is to be hoped that the core of this beautiful Therry tradition will continue.

In his early colonial years, Therry was acutely aware of the lack of the type of religious literature that was readily available in his homeland. It is typical of him that he addressed this need by putting pen to paper himself, laboriously chiselling out short articles that expressed the basics of the faith in language that children and semi-literate adults could easily follow. These, with a compendium of the most frequently used Catholic prayers, he published in book form. It was an imaginative measure which proved very useful at that time, when little else was available. He also obtained from abroad small individual tracts expressing the dogmas of the faith in easily readable language. These he reprinted in NSW and distributed to parents and others whom he felt could assist him in his teaching role.

Therry used to respond to some of the exaggerations and misinformation popping up in the secular press from time to time. Keeping a weather eye open for this kind of material, he acted as a watchdog for the Catholic Church. Even when his good friend and benefactor, Governor Sir William Denison, published something about the Church that Therry felt wasn't according to Hoyle, as it were, he took him to task forthwith in the *Sydney Morning Herald* — with utmost sensitivity and deference, of course. At the same time he sent him a letter with a tract entitled, "Sixty reasons in favour of the old religion", together with one of his own hymns for children.

The letter to the *Herald* exemplifies well Therry's tendency to impetuosity, to jump the gun, to leap before looking! As Denison pointed out in a very friendly letter to Therry when he returned the "Sixty reasons," all he had said in the original article was that the Christian Churches of the 19th century were not fully in tune with the pattern set by the Apostolic Church as described in the New Testament — a matter that could be lamented but hardly objected to by any of the Christian Churches.

As it transpired, Therry had no sooner read the original article "late last night" than his well-used pen went into action before he had a chance for second thoughts! This spontaneity, this type of impulsive response, was an attractive Therry characteristic and often quite an effective one, but it also got him into lots of trouble. He tended to be first off the mark, quick on the draw. For this he suffered and sometimes caused suffering to others.

His misreading of Denison's article didn't in any way diminish their friendship — a friendship that seemed to blossom on the mainland. When Denison was Governor of Van Diemen's Land Therry clashed with him frequently. Both Therry and Willson disagreed strongly with his attitude towards the Young Ireland prisoners, whom he wanted treated as common criminals in every way. Thanking Therry for the hymn for children, Denison graciously felt "it breathes a truly Catholic and loving spirit, a spirit which it is my earnest wish and prayer should animate us all in our relation to God and to our brethren".

That relationship to God and others is the key to a happy life, but it is complex and difficult, and many wise people seek help with it, whether from counsellors or directors or whoever. This is an important aspect of pastoral care nowadays. Most dioceses have trained experts to help people through bad patches and/or free them to grow emotionally and spiritually. Letters in the Therry papers indicate that he filled this role for a large number of people. Having no specialised training, he relied on commonsense, experience and God's guidance. The many ardent expressions of thanks indicate that he calmed an extraordinary number of storms and brought many battered and bruised souls to the safety and shelter of the divine harbour. Many years after the first Sisters of Charity arrived in Sydney, he was the one chosen as their Spiritual Director, a very important post indeed.

In the difficult and lonely struggle to preserve their own identity and charism as religious Sisters of Charity against a certain amount of pressure to include them in the Benedictine dream, Therry was always there for them, with wise counsel and material help when needed.

The relationship that caused most storms in the fledgling colony was the domestic one. The convict system itself, with its concomitant separations and general brutalising of people, had a stressful effect on the husband/wife/children unit. This, together with the generally hot humid conditions, led to abuse of alcohol, which was widespread among the poor and very damaging to families. Therry's frequent calls to mediate in family disputes convinced him that the husband/wife relationship was the all-important one and everything possible should be done to strengthen it.

Conversely, any attempt to weaken it should be resisted strongly. When in the 1850s he got wind of divorce legislation being under consideration by the Legislative Council, he was on his toes immediately. He didn't just dash off a letter, as was his normal reaction. This was much too serious for just one protesting clerical voice. Feeling that this demanded a unique and imaginative approach, he took what might be considered a late 20th-century approach — he had recourse to "people power"; he took up a petition! He organised nearly 100 representative families in Balmain and district to sign a document of protest. This document expressed great regret and alarm that such legislation would even be contemplated: "It is not the expressed will of the people and furthermore and especially it will be attended with great social and moral evils to the people of the colony at large". It goes on to point out that there will be times when separation of spouses will be appropriate, but to facilitate the dissolution of the all-important marriage bond itself by legislation "would be both dangerous and unwise".

The petition didn't succeed, but maybe it did have the effect of making access to the resultant divorce legislation limited and difficult. Therry, of course, foresaw that this would be the thin end of the wedge. It's only as we enter the third millennium that the full effects of that, and subsequent, divorce liberalisation are being realised. As well as the extreme trauma and violence often resulting from decisions about custody and access to children, the trauma to the children themselves is only recently becoming fully apparent.

Whereas up to now the accepted wisdom was that some children do suffer from the divorce of their parents, the latest scientific research is much more forthright in indicating that the suffering pretty well involves all the children. So much is this the accepted wisdom that counsellors are tending to advise parents to try to reconcile their differences for the sake of the children, if for no other reason — at least until the children come of age. It's good to know that the old pioneer, who was there with his people when the first incision was being made in the dam wall, did his best to alert the powers-that-be that the resulting trickle would eventually become a veritable torrent.

22

CAROLINE CHISHOLM'S FRIEND

Building up the family unit in country NSW was to become the focus of the work of an extraordinary woman called Caroline Chisholm, who arrived in Sydney from India with her husband, Major Archie Chisholm, and family in September 1838, just as Therry had left for Van Diemen's Land. Hearing so much about the pioneer priest from all sorts of people, she regretted missing the chance to meet and consult with him. Fortunately, she did meet him three years later in July 1841 when Therry made an unexpected visit. According to Mary Hoban, his return caused great excitement in Sydney Town. Word of his arrival spread like wildfire.

"It's Father Therry!", "It's Father Therry!", people shouted. "He's back from Van Diemen's Land!" They could hardly believe it, it was almost too good to be true. Older people were ecstatic. "Oh Father Therry, Father Therry ..." they repeated over and over, in surprise and excitement and joy. Young people surrounded him with cries of delight. (p 43) It was as if absence had even added to the fondness for him in people's hearts!

It was in this context that Caroline Chisholm met him for the first time. She found him a mine of wisdom and knowledge and very much au fait with the problem she was seeking to address. He seemed to know country NSW like one of the explorers. She told him how that very year she had

> in St Mary's Chapel made an offering of my talents
> to the God who gave them. I promised to know
> neither country nor creed but to serve all justly and

impartially ... I felt my offering was accepted and that God's blessing was on my work, but it was his will to permit many serious difficulties ...

It was at this time that Caroline took into her heart the deepest measure of responsibility for social injustice:

When I heard of a poor girl suffering distress and losing her reputation in consequence, I felt that I was not clear of guilt for I did not do all I could to prevent it. (Hoban, pp 43–44)

From 1841 on, Therry and Mrs Chisholm had found in each other, at the deepest level of spirit, soul friends. It was a friendship that was to persevere throughout their active lives.

Her efforts to brighten the predominantly masculine culture in the settlements he knew so well around Yass, Bathurst and Maitland with a hopeful gentler female one delighted him. He knew at first hand that it was almost impossible for ex-convicts who were making good on the land to fulfil their dream of finding a partner and raising a family. He applauded Caroline's imaginative and successful efforts to make this possible for so many of them. From what he heard of her work for the impoverished and exploited "Bounty girls", the attacks made on her by JD Lang and others, her incessant horse rides to all parts of NSW, her capacity to rough it and sleep with her charges under the stars — in all that he could see many parallels with his own earlier days.

When after all her amazing work — literally thousands settled securely in the bush — Caroline returned to Sydney from Victoria in the late 1850s impoverished and broken in health, her thoughts, according to O'Corrigan, turned to the friend of the outcast and the poor: "Dear Father Therry, if you can favour me with a call I shall be grateful to see you. I am too ill to leave my room." Therry was surprised to find her almost at death's door and, although he had a pressing engagement at Parramatta, he put it off as long as possible so that he could stay with her. She wrote to him again on July 12th 1858 announcing, "The inflammation has abated and I am much better". The purpose of the letter was a request for money: "Can you for a short time lend me fourteen or twenty pounds?"

Therry was saddened that this intrepid battler for the little people was thus reduced and friendless in a little house in Redfern. On receiving the money she wrote: "Your thoughtful arrangement is so like you and adds so much to your kindness in meeting my needs." The 'arrangement' she referred to had to do with the way of repaying the loan. He told her not to pay it back to himself but to give it to St Patrick's (anonymously) whenever or however she desired. Thus he made sure the repayment or non-repayment didn't in any way interfere with their friendship.

It was at this very time that the agitation between Deniehy and his followers and Polding and Gregory regarding the role of the laity and other matters of Church administration were at their height. Therry was deeply involved, having been asked by Polding to be, as Polding saw it, a dove among the hawks.

At the celebrated meeting in Campbelltown that same month, the plight of Mrs Chisholm and the way she seemed to have been abandoned by the Sydney Church (as well as by the Government) must have been weighing heavily on him, making it almost impossible for him to be other than on the side of the laity.

The neglect of Caroline Chisholm by the clergy of St Mary's continued to such an extent that JK Heydon (publisher of the *Freemans Journal*) wrote an urgent letter to Therry in May 1859:

> She has lately lost her eldest son by death in Victoria and I believe with him her principal means of existence for, if I understand the matter rightly, the Major, her husband, sold his commission to start his children in business. Ill as she is she is endeavouring to support herself by giving lessons in English to Chinamen at 1/6 per lesson and also by working for confectioners. They have young children at home

and have pawned a medal given her by His Holiness, to get bread for them ...

He concludes:

Now that the Archdeacon [McEncroe] is away I know no one but yourself to apply to in such a case.

Therry's response must have brought great comfort and healing because she made an amazing, although temporary, recovery. In less than two months, she was giving a public lecture on the Land Question and Manhood Suffrage in the Prince of Wales Theatre, Sydney. By December 1859 the Empire newspaper began to serialise her novelette, "Little Joe". Among other things she used the novelette to side with Deniehy against Polding on the thorny question of government funding. "The foot of the missionary has never been found in a Government shoe" was one of her memorable lines. She also challenged the clergy of the day, especially the Catholic clergy, for lacking zeal and commitment in ministering to their people. (As O'Corrigan observes, the old pioneer wasn't included in this.)

Her amazing work in the colony came to a fitting close when she opened an all-girls' school just before returning to England where she died in 1877.

Therry, who seemed to have an amazingly keen eye for observing situations of need, often came up with rather imaginative ways of addressing them. When, for example, he became aware of the overcrowded and very poor living conditions at the Good Shepherd/Sisters of Charity convent, he took up his faithful pen and wrote to none other than Lady Denison, the wife of the Governor. He suggested cleverly that she might like to take up their cause and even become their patrona! As such she could bring their plight to the attention of her husband, the one person who could open parliamentary doors, especially the one allocating grants! He also pointed out to Lady Denison that the sisters "could do ten times more good than they can now effect, if they could obtain the use for two or three hours of one or two days every week of a plain carriage". O'Sullivan goes on to remark:

It is interesting that it is Therry and not the Archbishop or his Vicar-General, though officially responsible for the nuns, who realized how their work was hampered by lack of transport. (p 201)

Another problem, an overseas one this time, that had long preoccupied the old priest and came to a head in the late 1850s, concerned the Maoris in New Zealand. Their treatment by the white settlers, like the treatment of the Aborigines in NSW, disturbed him very much. He was in touch with his good friend Bishop Pompallier who, in turn, was well known and respected by the Maori Chiefs. When the Maori war broke out in 1860, Pompallier, finding himself helpless to bring about a rapprochement between the Chiefs and the colonial authorities, appealed to his Australian colleague for help. Therry again thought of his friend in high places, this time contacting the Governor directly. He pointed out that he, Denison, might be the one person with the stature and influence to convince the Queen and the New Zealand authorities to overlook the tragic blood-spilling and reaffirm the 1840 treaty of Waitangi. If they were willing to do this, Therry volunteered to join the Bishop in New Zealand in what he anticipated would be a successful bid to get a majority of the Chiefs to respond likewise.

It would seem that Therry's empathy with native peoples was known to at least some of the Chiefs, who would have welcomed his and Pompallier's intervention.

Some months before he died, Therry made a final appeal, perhaps urged on by his friend in New Zealand. He drafted a letter to Sir John O'Shannassy of Melbourne, reminding him of the problems across the Tasman and the sad plight of the Maori people. He suggested that Sir John write to the different governments in Australia and ask them to use their influence with the Queen and the Government in New Zealand on behalf of the Maoris. Is it not possible that this concern and activity had some small influence on bringing about the peace that eventuated some time later?

23

HE DIES IN HARNESS

Early in the morning of May 24th 1864, the Balmain church bell rang out unexpectedly. It was not a Sunday; so it must be a summons for parishioners to assemble for some reason other than Mass. As they shuffled out of their houses and along the narrow streets to St Augustine's Church, they felt instinctively that it must be bad news. It was indeed — worse than they had ever anticipated. Their beloved pastor, John Joseph Therry, had died during the night!

It was a great shock. The day before, in his usual good health, he had attended a garden party at Government House and chatted with all and sundry, as was his wont. That evening after Benediction, he had participated in an event that he had long been looking forward to and preparing for. He believed people needed something to draw them together and give them a sense of belonging and fraternity. From his experience elsewhere, he knew the establishment of the Guild of St Mary and St Joseph would achieve this. However, he didn't like imposing things on people from above; they themselves had to want it, had to be convinced of the need and the way to meet that need. When that happened, the night of May 23rd was set aside for the inauguration ceremony. It was the climax of a lot of hard work for Therry and, just as when 42 years earlier he had blessed the foundation stone of St Mary's Chapel, which Macquarie had laid, he was in his element. So important was this to him that he had said only a few days before that he would die content once the Guild was established!

(That very night these two events took place, and all the indications are that he was very content.)

He had remained happily at the ceremony until his 10 pm return to the presbytery, where he prepared for bed. About midnight he felt cold, colder than he'd ever felt in the Southern Highlands or even in Hobart, a cold that somehow was submerging him. Although he wasn't unfamiliar with crisis situations, feeling that this was the big one, he naturally thought of his best friend. He called his servant and asked him to send for Fr (now Archdeacon) McEncroe. While the messenger was on his way, the sick man asked that the prayers of the dying be recited, he himself joining in with obvious faith and confidence.

Then the end came. Before his old friend could reach the bedside, Fr Therry lay back on his pillow, closed his eyes and, with the hint of an expectant smile on his face, died without drama or struggle. Somehow, it was fitting that he should die in harness. From the day of his arrival in Sydney till the day of his death, he had hardly stopped; he had been active to the last.

During the days and nights when his body lay exposed for public veneration, at first in St Augustine's, Balmain and then in St Mary's Cathedral, people queued up in unprecedented numbers to pay their respects. As at the laying of the foundation stone of St Mary's way back in 1821, so now, the powerful of the land and the lowly, the rulers and the ruled, the Catholic and the Protestant, the convict and the free, the Governor and the Archbishop . . . they came, many in tears, to honour him.

Archdeacon McEncroe's panegyric was described as "the outpouring of his heart's love over the remains of one who had been his dearest friend". Many times his voice faltered and broke and he was joined in his sorrow by the crowd. He traced Therry's life from the day he landed "in the vast continent committed solely to his care". He pointed to the present vast organisation of 1864, and to the beautiful Cathedral itself as Therry's monument. (Birchley, p 260)

returning children, whose moral weakness might require its relaxation.

This "Therry" approach has been to a great extent the distinctive Aussie approach of the pastors who have succeeded him. They gave it recent practical expression in Rome at the Synod of Oceania towards the end of 1998. Many of the Australian Bishops present called for an altering of the discipline of the Church to allow, for example, divorced and remarried Catholics to approach the table of the Eucharist; similarly, to make the Eucharist available to believing Christians of other Churches who desire to join in celebrating Mass; to welcome back to the active ministry priests who have married ... In this the Bishops were responding to the *sensus fidelium*, the perceived wishes of many committed Australian Catholics. The inflexible response from officialdom in Rome to these matters of Church discipline would have made little sense to Therry and most of those who succeeded him in the Australian Church. His is an inheritance too precious to be allowed to slip through pastoral fingers, especially at this time when the role of conscience is being wound back and pre-Vatican II style legalism and orthodoxy is being strongly promoted.

In death as in life, an extraordinary number of people loved Fr Therry: the sick and the lonely, the victim of injustice, the convict and the orphan, the condemned awaiting execution, the battler trying to get on top of things, ordinary men and women trying to build a decent life in the far-away Antipodes — they all had every reason to love and venerate this so very human and fallible, compassionate and hot-headed priest, who had the pugnacity and the obstinacy needed to take on their cause, fight their battles and stand beside them in their hour of need.

When Therry's oldest and best friend John McEncroe died, Henry Kendall composed some verses in his honour, some of which apply to each of these two greats of the early Australian Church. It seems fitting to let the Protestant colonial poet have the last say:

His ways were light because he loved
His suffering peers apart from sect:
A silent power by trouble proved
and made elect.

For searching to the core of things
He found the sign that made him strong
While we who sigh like seaside reeds
Do look and long.

The deep divinity which rests
For ever at the root of things
Was shown to him who stood the tests
of sufferings.

And seeing beauty hid beneath
The dust of dogmas evermore
He learned its speech, and came to know
what life is for.

EPILOGUE

It may be of some value to compare the way of faith brought to New Holland by John Joseph Therry in the 1820s and that brought by me, 125 years later, in the 1940s. Between those years, great changes occurred, especially in Ireland, changes which had a profound effect on the way people related to God, to the Church and to the world. The spirituality young Therry imbibed at his mother's knee, as it were, and later on from his other mother, his alma mater, St Patrick's College, Carlow, still had a flavour which was just about lost when I came of age. The flavour came from his Celtic roots. The Book of Kells on display at the National Gallery of Australia during the early months of the year 2000 dates back to 9th century Ireland. The designs and decorations of its beautiful artwork reflect the patterns on the famous High Crosses that can still be seen at Clonmacnoise and other ancient places. It is an indication of the existence of a unique Celtic way of being Christian which flourished in Ireland after St Patrick. It began to change when Rome set up diocese in the 11th century. The Ireland of the late 1700s, however, still retained and treasured some of the old Celtic ways. Especially, during the Penal Laws' era, when all overt religious practices were banned, the Celtic flavour helped people to cope and to survive till some measure of freedom was restored towards the end of the 18th century.

Efforts had been made by priests trained on the Continent to replace the old Celtic religious practices with those imported from Europe but, because of the political situation, they were mostly ineffectual. That a strong residue of the Celtic Christian culture remained in Therry is evident in his favouring of the more mystical books of the Bible, like the Wisdom books of the Old Testament and the Gospel of John; in his strong preference for singing and music; and in his leaning towards the poetic.

By the time the big push for the Europeanisation of the Irish Church came, Therry was well settled in the Antipodes. The push was spearheaded by Paul Cullen who, as Cardinal Archbishop of Dublin from 1852 until his death in 1878, exercised enormous influence in bringing the Irish Church into tandem with its Continental counterpart. The Catechism of the Council of Trent, rather than the scriptures, became *de rigueur* for pastors and teachers; the boundaries of dioceses and parishes were tightly delineated; and Catholic life was strictly brought into line with the decrees of Canon Law, the Statutes of Vatican Council 1, the Synods of Thurles (1852) and Maynooth (1875). Practices that were typically Celtic and ideally suited to the Irish temperament were frowned on. Pilgrimages, for example, were discouraged.

The Irish loved travelling together to shrines or holy wells or other such places associated with local saints, where worship and praise were often interspersed with song and dance, story and fun. (At times and in some circumstances, alcohol was available and consumed to excess.) This involving of the whole person, the body as well as the spirit, came naturally to them. It made them aware of their oneness with the natural world and the goodness of creation.

With little regard for the people or their culture, European ways of religious expression were fostered and developed. Pious devotional practices from the Continent were thought to be more up to date and sophisticated than the old Gaelic language practices that were still in vogue, especially in rural areas. A whole plethora of devotions were imported and became enormously popular. Among them: Sacred Heart devotions, Nine First Fridays, 40 hours devotion, Parish Missions ... Novenas of all kinds proliferated, as did scapulars, medals, Rosary beads, holy pictures, books of prayers like the "Key of Heaven" and the "Garden of the Soul", "the Imitation of Christ" and many more. To miss Sunday Mass became a grave sin, as did breaches of the Friday abstinence and the Lenten Fast and of course sexual sins could never be other than grave. Catholic life, in fact, became a matter of obedience to concrete rules and regulations. Spiritual growth and perfection tended to be measured in terms of doing rather than being, of quantity rather than quality.

The centrality of the church building was emphasised. The Nuptial Mass and the Funeral Mass were to be celebrated there, rather than in the family home as was the custom. In Irish seminaries, theology and *lectio divina* were based on books obtained from the Continent, as were the doctrinal points used for discursive meditation. The old Celtic love of scripture and especially Bible stories was frowned on as being somewhat Protestant. The mystical gave way to a more rational, literal, black and white view of reality, with little or no hint of grey or the mysterious or the legendary, so dear to the Celts.

In all this, however, Catholic life flourished, the Church became strong and even a tad triumphalistic. The downside was the loss of the more free and easy, relaxed, communitarian way of the past. The poetic, the imaginative, the musical gave way to a more prosaic literalism.

As Tomas Uasal de Bhal noted:

> One is loath to be critical of so venerable a corpus of prayer and piety, but may one most respectfully suggest that it may be too sustained where it should be more spontaneous, too civilised and urban where it should be a bit bedraggled and daring and rural, too elaborate where it should be inspired, too flat and level where it should be soaring to the skies, too articulate and too fully stated for the Celtic mentality, for which, as Kuno Myer said, the half-said thing is dearest.(O'Riordan, pp 69–70)

Roman culture, that had such an influence on the Church in Europe, never spread to Ireland. There the culture remained Celtic. The Church quickly adapted to it and, in the process, raised it to a new level of learning and spirituality.

As Timothy Joyce puts it:

> The Celtic Church, never fully part of the Roman culture and civilisation, preserved a sense of its own local identity. The Celtic tradition was very communal, expressing a horizontal equality and de-emphasising vertical hierarchical differences. Men and women tended to be more equal than in the Roman experience. Clergy and lay people were closer. The Bishop was primarily an evangeliser leading his priests in works of spreading the Gospel, but he remained a member of the local community, of which an abbot was the administrative head. Together, the Christian Community practised (or aimed at practising) a holistic spirituality that embraced the mind (respect for learning, preserving the tradition in writing), the heart (nature, poetry, music) and body (penance and pilgrimage). It was a mystical spirituality that avoided later dualisms by seeing the sacred and the secular as one ... Celtic Christians recognised the authority of the Pope, though not subserviently. They rather trusted their own experience and respected their own particular gifts as worthy to share with a larger Church. (pp 150–151)

In Therry's time, some of this vision of the local Church still survived. It had all but disappeared in mine. Therry saw the Church as incardinating itself in the local milieu, sensitive to the circumstances and characteristics of the local people. The fact that New Holland was a penal colony, as well as a newly developing country (as far as white people were concerned), had to be reflected in the spirituality and religious life of the people. The uniqueness of the Great South Land, its enormous distances, its great deserts and empty outback, its droughts and floods and occasional cyclones, its dispossessed Aborigines and legions of convicts had to be factored in when developing an Australian way of being "Church".

That an Australian Church should be an exact replica of the western European model would be anathema to Therry — unfortunately, not to me. Having escaped the Cullen-inspired Europeanising of the Irish Church, he could follow a more relaxed agenda. His vision wedded, in a more or less equal proportion, the natural and the supernatural; the world of New Holland — so unique, so different, so beautiful — with the infinitely rich world of God's inexhaustible grace. He was familiar with the call (first addressed to the men of Judah): "yours to drive a new furrow" (Jeremiah 4:3); the call to cultivate a new spiritual plant that was at home in the Antipodes — one that was in union with the universal Church, but not shedding the unique colours and vitality arising out of the fruitfulness of the new furrow.

Unfortunately, the Irish clergy who followed him, like myself, having lost that old Celtic vision, were tutored in another model, the Irish-Roman one, which measured the perfection of the local Church by its approximation to the Roman model. Vatican Council II, surprisingly enough, affirmed the old Celtic view, bringing back the concept of the local Church not as an inferior branch, but as the universal Church incardinated in and adapted to this particular milieu. It modified the First Vatican Council's centralising of papal authority by an emphasis on the traditional authority of local Bishops, and recognised the collegial authority of Pope and Bishops acting together. The local Bishop was no longer to be seen as a minor player, but as a full member of the Apostolic College with the Pope.

Thus did the Council seek to preserve the diversity and richness of local culture, local rites and local customs. Regretfully, this has been watered down in recent years. When the Roman curia sees some un-Roman practices taking hold, as it did in Australia towards the end of the second millennium, it gets uneasy and proceeds to ease the local Church back into line. The "Statement of Conclusions" issued in December 1998, for example, was a strong call to the Australian Church to toe the party line.

In his capacity to see the sacred in the secular, mentioned above, Therry was much more gifted than I. He escaped, at least partially, the dualistic attitude that had come full circle in my time; the attitude that divides the divine from the human, the natural from the supernatural, heaven from earth. He retained much of the Celtic Sacramental outlook which saw all that is, in all its wonderful diversity, as a living theophany, a living manifestation of Christ, the Word. The ordinary, the everyday, the human is the seat of God's presence.

The Incarnation is not just a doctrine, it is something to be lived and savoured in all aspects of life. The divine reality is now to be found within every creature — enlivening, empowering, directing. God is not controlling in an external determinate way, but is within, calling, liberating, comforting ... He was amazed to find that aboriginal spirituality paralleled his own in significant ways. Especially in the aboriginal attachment to the land and to all natural phenomena, he saw a reflection of something deeply embedded in his own Celtic roots. This perhaps goes some way towards explaining the unique rapport of Therry (and his friend John McEncroe) with the Aborigines.

Therry's God is like St Patrick's God and indeed the God of the Aborigines:

God of heaven and earth, seas and rivers
God of sun and moon and all the stars
God of high mountains and lowly valleys
God over heaven, in heaven and under heaven ...

In the psalms Therry, like his distant forebears, found a way of "singing to the Lord with all the earth" as in Psalm 95:

O sing to the Lord all the earth ...
Let the heavens rejoice and earth be glad
let the sea and all within it thunder praise
let the land and all it bears rejoice
all the trees of the land shout for joy
at the presence of the Lord for he comes ...

or again, Psalm 65:

Cry out with joy to God all the earth
— say to God how tremendous your deeds ...
or Psalm 23:
The Lord's is the earth and its fullness
the world and all its peoples.
Or the Book of Judith:
Let all your creatures serve you
for you spoke and they were made.
You sent forth your spirit and it formed them
There is none can resist your voice. (16:13)

In this creation-centred, imaginative spirituality, the world is filled with a new richness. As Elizabeth Barrett Browning, meditating on the Burning Bush (Exodus 3:2), put it, "Earth's crammed with Heaven, and every common bush afire with God". But not everyone is aware: "only he who sees, takes off his shoes, the rest sit round it and pluck blackberries." (Aurora Leigh)

Therry was one of those who had the mystic's eyes that could see the unseen, as did the Irish patriot awaiting execution in Easter week 1916:

I see his blood upon the rose
And in the sky the glory of his eyes,
His body gleams amid eternal snows
His tears fall from the skies.
The thunder and the singing of the birds
are but his voice ...
Rocks are his written words.
All pathways by his feet are worn,
His strong heart stirs the ever-beating sea,
His crown of thorns is twined with every thorn,
His cross is every tree. (Joseph Mary Plunkett)

According to Karl Rahner SJ, the great theologian who believes future Christians will survive as such only by being mystics, having those eyes to see the unseen and the ears to hear the silent music is all-important.

When I came to Sydney during World War II, I was surprised and in some ways delighted to find Australia so different from the country I'd left — so much so that it took quite an effort to adapt to the new scene, the new culture, the new relaxed way of life. However, I had no trouble adapting to the religious scene. In most ways it was remarkably like the one I'd left. Those who had come before me had done a very successful job in transporting the Irish model of Church to the Antipodes. But, as we saw, the Church that had developed in Ireland from the 1840s on was not Irish, but western European. That's the model the Irish clergy and religious and laity brought with them.

The old Celtic model had all but disappeared after the Great Famine. This has not been well understood by people who blame the "Irishness" of the Australian Church for perceived weaknesses in facing the challenges of the new millennium. In fact, the European model established by the Irish has been a great advantage in the multicultural society that Australia has become. Catholics who arrived from Continental Europe in huge numbers after World War II found it relatively easy to fit into the Australian Church. Apart from the problem of language and consequent community involvement, it was very like what they were used to in Europe.

Conversely, it was far more difficult for those who migrated to America. There the problem of settling in was much more difficult, resulting, in fact, in the creation of a new structure of national Churches.

Although Therry's religion and spirituality was Roman and Tridentine in many ways, growing up towards the end of the Penal Laws' era, he imbibed, as we saw, a viable portion of the old traditional Irish spiritual diet. This he and his convict contemporaries brought to New Holland. It nourished the fledgling Church down under for many years, and was inclusive enough to allow a supplementary Benedictine recipe to become part of the spiritual menu with it, but it eventually succumbed to the stronger and maybe more sustaining religious fare coming through the increasing number of Romanised Irish and English migrants.

At the core of Therry's spirituality was his vision of God, a vision based on scripture, for which he had a great love. Beautiful images like the Good Shepherd going in search of the lost sheep and bringing it back joyfully on his shoulder, or the loving, forgiving father rushing out to embrace the prodigal, sinful son, resonated deeply in the Celtic soul. This was a God who passionately loved his people. So much so that even when they strayed away and left him, he welcomed them back with open arms — no conditions, no strings attached, no demand for further punishment. My God likewise loved and forgave his people, but not without some strings attached. The strings are evident in a beautiful practice that came to Ireland from France after the Great Famine. Called devotion to the Sacred Heart, the Irish embraced it with enthusiasm. The Sacred Heart image became part of the décor of just about every Irish home, as indeed it did here in Australia in my early days.

It was a constant reminder of the love of God revealed in the human heart of Jesus. The heart, however, was pierced and there was a certain pained look in the face of Jesus. This expressed another and maybe the principal aspect of the devotion. God has been offended by human sins, he has been hurt, and we need to win back his love, to earn his forgiveness — in other words, to make reparation.

Making reparation or satisfaction was further emphasised through the various Marian apparitions, especially at Fatima in Portugal in 1917. Satisfaction had to be made, too, for the poor souls in purgatory, otherwise they could spend next to forever in pain and suffering.

This seems to picture a God more in tune with that depicted in parts of the Hebrew Scriptures, a disappointed and almost angry God, who has to be placated. Although this may have been spiritually nourishing for many people, it was quite alien to the Celtic way of thinking and somewhat at variance with the New Testament image of God so dear to Therry and his convict flock.

That the New Testament God was Trinitarian brought much more joy to Therry than it did to me. To him it was much more than an abstract mystery that one had to accept as a sign of one's Christian commitment. Early in my time, Karl Rahner SJ decried the fact that the Trinity had become rather irrelevant to most Christians. He acutely observed that if the Church changed the doctrine from three to two or four persons in God, it would make little difference to believing people. To Therry however (and increasingly to the present-day post-Vatican II Church), the Trinity was very relevant. A God of relationships, of love and intimacy, of eternal sharing, of giving and receiving is, indeed, good news for human beings made in God's image.

Whenever he encountered loving, caring relationships, which wasn't infrequent even in a convict situation, Therry was getting a dim but very real glimpse of the giving and receiving, the loving and sharing going on at a macro level in the Triune Godhead. Good human interaction, especially with lots of stories, music, singing and dancing, could be seen in Celtic eyes to reflect, in a small everyday way, the mysterious divine relating among the persons of the Godhead. Because community came naturally to the Celts, they readily tuned into the Trinitarian community.

Being communitarian almost by nature, one could say, they never suffered from the excessive individualism, the "Jesus and me" type of spirituality that became so much in vogue in my time. The Vatican II vision of Church as "Communio" would resonate with them as it would have with Therry. Being communitarian gave the Celt an awareness of being one's brother's keeper, of being responsible for others, of seeking justice and fair play — an awareness that was so much stronger in Therry than in me. Celtic Christianity was close to the elements, to God, to homelessness and, often as well, to poverty and starvation:

> The Celtic peoples have undergone oppression, suffering and progressive marginalisation. The mysticism that characterised the Celts is related to this. Only God was at the centre and really important. All else was secondary. One must not forget one's own poverty, limitations, sufferings and injustices. And from these one must reach out to the sufferings of others. Patrick never forgot the years he spent in slavery and

loneliness and he was the first European to speak out against slavery. (Joyce, p 156)

Therry's passionate reaching out to the convicts and the Aborigines and others who were marginalised and badly treated related to those deep spiritual roots that were still active in him but had, unfortunately, become quite atrophied by my time.

These roots, however, are not dead; they are still there, especially in people of Celtic origin. Happily, they are being rediscovered today by many western Christians who are seeking a spirituality more in tune with the contemporary world view, which emphasises the interconnectedness of all creation and the need for ecological care and responsibility. Recently emerging interest in Eastern mysticism and meditation is also contributing to the resurgence of the Celtic way. To meet the challenges of today's world, many people are finding that the European spiritual diet brought to Australia mainly by Irish clergy and religious like myself needs to be supplemented by the more environmentally friendly Celtic one brought mainly by John Joseph Therry.

I will conclude with WB Yeats and George McLeod. McLeod recreated St Columba's Missionary Community in Iona in Scotland in relatively recent times. He has done much to revive Celtic Christianity as a living spirituality that speaks to our scientifically conscious and ecologically aware age. As Ian Bradley writes:

> Totally opposed to the dualism and narrow anthropocentrism of contemporary western Christianity, he [McLeod] preached "whole salvation" rather than "soul salvation". His strong sense of a truly Cosmic Christ present throughout nature was influenced by eastern theology and scientific theory, but it is surely the distinctive note of Celtic spirituality which echoes most clearly through his prayers:
> "Invisible we see you, Christ beneath us,
> with earthly eyes we see beneath us stones and
> dust and dross,
> fit subjects the analyst's table.

But with the eye of faith, we know you uphold.
In you all things consist and hang together:
The very atom is light energy,
the grass is vibrant,
the rocks pulsate.
All is in flux, turn but a stone and an angel moves.
Underneath are the everlasting arms.
Unknowable we know you, Christ beneath us."
(Bradley, pp 107–8).

In many of his poems William Butler Yeats expresses a
spirituality that is typically Celtic.

I, proclaiming that there is
Among birds or beasts or men
One that is perfect or at peace,
Danced on Cruachan's windy plain,
Upon Cro-Patrick sang aloud;
All that could run or leap or swim
Whether in wood, water, or cloud,
Acclaiming, proclaiming, declaiming Him.

BIBLIOGRAPHY

▶ Birchley, Delia, 1986 *John McEncroe*. Collins Dove.

▶ Bonwick, James, 1902. *An Octogenarian's Reminiscences*. J Nicholas, London.

▶ Bradley, Ian, 1993. *The Celtic Way*. Darton, Longman & Todd, London.

▶ Campion, Edmund, 1984. *John Joseph Therry*. Faith and Culture.

▶ Carnagie, Margaret, 1973. *Friday Mount*. Hawthorn Press, Melbourne.

▶ Clark, Manning, 1968. *A History of Australia* (Vols I & II). Melbourne University Press.

▶ Clune, Frank, 1948. *Wild Colonial Boys*. Angus & Robertson, Sydney.

▶ Colonial Papers, 1787 and 1791. Public Records Office, London.

▶ Comerford, Rev M, 1883. *Collections Diocese of Kildare & Leighlin*, (Vol 1). Duffy Publications, Dublin.

▶ Costello, Con, *Botany Bay*. Extracts from *The Word* magazine, February 1988.

▶ Cullen, Rev JH, 1949–53. *Bishop Willson*. ACR.

▶ Donovan, Finbarr. Professor of History, National University of Ireland, Dublin. Researched but unpublished works on Therry's Irish connections.

▶ Eddy, Rev J SJ, 1964. *Talk on John Joseph Therry*. ACHS.

▶ Hoban, Mary, 1984. *Fifty-one Pieces of Wedding Cake*. Polding Press, Sydney.

▶ Joyce, Timothy OSA, 1998. *Celtic Christianity*. Orbis Books, New York.

▶ Keneally, Thomas, 1998. *The Great Shame*. Random House, Australia.

▶ Kennedy, Ted, 2000. *Who is Worthy*. Pluto Press, Sydney.

▶ Kennedy, Fr T. 117 Redfern St, Redfern. Researched but as yet unpublished works used in several chapters. Much of the facts and quotes regarding Dan Denehy, Frank McNamara, Connor Wholohan and others has come from this source.

▶ Kiernan, TJ, 1954. *The Irish Exiles in Australia*. Burnes Oates, Melbourne.

SIGNIFICANT DATES

1790 John Joseph Therry born in Cork.

1789 Rebellion of United Irishmen.

1800 Convict priests Harold, Dixon and O'Neill transported to Sydney.

1803 Father Dixon celebrates first Mass in colony (May 15).

1804 Castle Hill uprising. Dixon's Mass banned.

1813 Blaxland, Wentworth and Lawson succeed in getting over the Blue Mountains.

1815 Therry ordained priest.

1817 Father Jeremiah O'Flynn's arrival.

1818 Father Jeremiah O'Flynn's deportation.

1820 Fathers Therry and Conolly arrive in Sydney (May 3).

1821 Conolly to Van Diemen's Land.

1821 Therry and Macquarie lay foundation stone of St Mary's Chapel (Oct 29).

1824 Hamilton Hume explores an overland route to Port Phillip Bay.

1825 Therry suspended as Chaplain.

1826 Father Power arrives.

1829 Roger Therry arrives.

1830 Power dies in Sydney.

1831 Father Dowling arrives.

1831 Roof on St Mary's Chapel.

1832 Father John McEncroe arrives, also JH Plunkett.

1833 Dr Ullathorne arrives.

1835 Bishop Polding arrives.

1835 Therry to Campbelltown.

1836 Governor Bourke's Church Act.

1837 Therry reinstated as Chaplain.

1838 Therry to Van Diemen's Land.

1839 Father Philip Conolly dies in Hobart.

1841 St Joseph's Church Hobart opened.

1844 Bishop Willson arrives in Hobart.

1846 Therry in Melbourne (temporary appointment).

1847 Therry in Windsor NSW (temporary appointment).

1854 Therry returns to Sydney, to St Patrick's Church.

1856 Therry appointed pastor of Balmain.
1858 Therry gets title of Archpriest.
1864 Therry dies in Balmain.
1868 John McEncroe dies in Sydney.
1877 Archbishop Polding dies in Sydney.
1901 Remains of Therry, Power, McEncroe and Polding transferred to St Mary's Cathedral, under the altar dedicated to the Irish Saints.
1948 Remains of all four re-interred in Cathedral Crypt.
2000 St Mary's Cathedral completed with spires.